Visual CBT

Using pictures to help you apply Cognitive Behaviour Therapy to change your life

Avy Joseph and Maggie Chapman

CAPSTONE

Cover design: Mackerel Ltd

This edition first published 2013
© 2013 Avy Joseph and Maggie Chapman

Registered office
Capstone Publishing Ltd. (A Wiley Company), John Wiley and Sons Ltd, The Atrium, Southern Gate, Chichester, West Sussex, PO19 8SQ, United Kingdom

For details of our global editorial offices, for customer services and for information about how to apply for permission to reuse the copyright material in this book please see our website at www.wiley.com.

The right of the authors to be identified as the authors of this work has been asserted in accordance with the Copyright, Designs and Patents Act 1988.

Reprinted May 2013

Wiley publishes in a variety of print and electronic formats and by print-on-demand. Some material included with standard print versions of this book may not be included in e-books or in print-on-demand. If this book refers to media such as a CD or DVD that is not included in the version you purchased, you may download this material at http://booksupport.wiley.com. For more information about Wiley products, visit www.wiley.com.

Designations used by companies to distinguish their products are often claimed as trademarks. All brand names and product names used in this book and on its cover are trade names, service marks, trademarks or registered trademarks of their respective owners. The publisher and the book are not associated with any product or vendor mentioned in this book. None of the companies referenced within the book have endorsed the book.

Limit of Liability/Disclaimer of Warranty: While the publisher and author have used their best efforts in preparing this book, they make no representations or warranties with respect to the accuracy or completeness of the contents of this book and specifically disclaim any implied warranties of merchantability or fitness for a particular purpose. It is sold on the understanding that the publisher is not engaged in rendering professional services and neither the publisher nor the author shall be liable for damages arising herefrom. If professional advice or other expert assistance is required, the services of a competent professional should be sought.

Library of Congress Cataloging-in-Publication Data

Joseph, Avy.
Visual CBT : Using pictures to help you apply Cognitive Behaviour Therapy to change your life / Avy Joseph and Maggie Chapman.
pages cm
Summary: "This will be first book in the UK to approach the powerful Cognitive Behavioural Therapy in an illustrated way. This innovative method will allow the reader to clearly understand and remember the concepts featured"– Provided by publisher.
ISBN 978-0-85708-354-8 (pbk.) – ISBN (invalid) 978-0-85708-352-4 (ebk) – ISBN 978-0-85708-353-1 (ebk) – ISBN 978-0-85708-351-7 (ebk)   1. Cognitive therapy.   2. Cognitive therapy–Pictorial works.
I. Champman, Maggie, 1954–   II. Title.
RC489.C63J674 2013
616.89'1425–dc23
2012045727

A catalogue record for this book is available from the British Library.

ISBN 978-0-857-08354-8 (pbk) ISBN 978-0-857-08352-4 (ebk)
ISBN 978-0-857-08353-1 (ebk) ISBN 978-0-857-08351-7 (ebk)

Set in 10/13.5 pt Adobe Caslon Pro by Toppan Best-set Premedia Limited
Printed in Great Britain by TJ International Ltd, Padstow, Cornwall, UK

Contents

Cognitive Behaviour Therapy: An Introduction

Why This Book? What Will You Get From It?

We train adults in a variety of cognitive and behavioural therapies. This includes one day workshops as well as longer term courses. We also run a private clinic working with adults on many issues including anxiety disorders, depression, relationship problems, trauma, psychosomatic issues such as irritable bowel syndrome and blushing to name but a few. Both our students and our clients learn how to understand and develop awareness of the different types of emotions we experience and how to change them in a constructive manner in order to make progress and to move on.

Understanding the different types of emotions we may feel, and knowing what is at the heart of these emotions, can be tricky at times, especially when we experience many at the same time.

This book is designed to help you make sense of your emotions using Cognitive Behaviour Therapy (CBT) displayed in a visual way. We believe that using illustrations to demonstrate how we think, what we tend to do, and do when we experience different emotions can be helpful to anyone who wants to use CBT in their life.

The aim of the book is to use visual techniques to help you understand:

- The different types of emotions we experience such as depression, sadness, anxiety, concern, anger, annoyance, guilt, remorse, hurt, disappointment, embarrassment/shame, regret, jealousy, concern for one's relationship, unhealthy envy and healthy envy.

- How to differentiate between what's an unhealthy and what's a healthy negative emotion or feeling.
- How to find out what is at the heart of these feelings and emotions.
- How to change and move on in a constructive way.

Before we get started there is something you need to know.

Emotional Responsibility – You are largely responsible for how you feel and act.

At the heart of almost all emotional and behavioural change is Emotional Responsibility. Your feelings and reactions are greatly influenced by the attitudes and beliefs that you currently hold as true. Some of those beliefs you hold, but no longer question, may be untrue and unhelpful to you.

Being 'largely' responsible does not mean that another person, situation or event sometimes causes your behaviour. What this means is that there are some disorders like Bipolar Depression that are organic in nature; meaning that it's to do with the person's biology or genetic makeup. To change how we feel, understanding Emotional Responsibility is very important.

The principle of Emotional Responsibility can be difficult to accept, particularly if you are going through a difficult time or have experienced a personal tragedy. It is natural to feel angry, sad, depressed or hurt in response to people, accidents, illness and other challenges in life. Notice that people feel and experience contrasting emotions when they experience the same problem. Therefore it is not the event or another person that **'makes'** you feel what you feel.

If it was true that events caused emotional responses or feelings, then everyone experiencing the same event would experience the same feeling BUT they don't. At the heart of your emotional experience are your beliefs.

How you think about something or someone is generally down to you. The consequential feelings and behaviours are also generally down to you. Uncomfortable, but generally true, nevertheless.

What is Cognitive Behaviour Therapy (CBT)?

The two pioneers of CBT, Albert Ellis and Aaron Beck, shared the view that most emotional problems arise from faulty thinking and that the remedy is found in corrective actions. Both approaches concentrate on *present* problems and *present* thinking, in contrast to the earlier forms of psychotherapy.

Both recommended the inclusion of behavioural exercises.

It's worth knowing a little more about the two main schools of Cognitive and Behavioural Therapies – you may decide that one works for you better than the other. Both have evidence-based theories and both have a structured framework and process of therapy. We have included a section explaining the Ellis and Beck models at the end of this book.

These two great thinkers have made an enormous contribution to the understanding and application of psychological health. We tend to prefer Ellis's model most of the time because of its philosophical basis. We find that it resonates both with our students and with our clients easily. This book is mainly influenced by Ellis's model but uses some aspects of Beck's model.

'People are disturbed not by things but by their view of things'

This often quoted phrase of Epictetus (Stoic philosopher) is at the heart of the Ellis model. The intent behind Ellis's work and his theory was to:

- Help people clarify their emotions, behaviour and goals.
- Identify the unhealthy beliefs that are at the heart of their emotional problems and that sabotage their goals.
- Dispute them and replace them with their healthier version in order to get better through consistent and constructive action.
- Finally, to generalise the change to other areas of life.

Epictetus's quote can be conceptualised by the ABC diagram which follows.

It is not the event, but the belief or view you hold about the event, which is at the heart of emotional states. Emotions, thoughts and behaviours can be healthy and functional, or unhealthy and dysfunctional. The event can be something that has happened in the **past**, something that is happening **now** or something that could happen in the **future**. It can also be real, imaginary, internal or external. Internal events can be thoughts, images, memories, physical sensations or emotions.

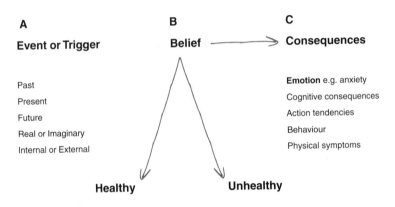

A is the event, **B** is the unhealthy or healthy belief you hold about **A** and **C** are the consequential responses which can be:

- Cognitive (thoughts and assumptions)
- Action tendencies (what you feel like doing)
- Behaviours (what you do)
- Emotions (anxiety, concern, depression etc.)
- Physical symptoms (blushing, heart racing etc.)

CBT is problem focused and practical – its aim is to help you get better in the long term, which is done through changing your unhealthy beliefs to their healthy counterparts. The process of change requires repetition, consistency and vigour in the application of the healthy beliefs. This means you will think and act in accordance with your healthy beliefs even though it will feel uncomfortable at first. It is completely natural as emotional change takes time and comes last after the change in thinking and behaviour. Understanding does not create emotional change. If you were to read a book on how to drive a car, understanding that does not transform you into a competent driver instantly. You would have to apply what you understand, i.e. getting into the car, accepting it will feel uncomfortable and challenging at first and mistakes can be made but by being determined and persistent you will begin to feel comfortable.

Unhealthy Beliefs

Beliefs that are unhealthy have, at their core, explicit or implicit, rigid, powerful demands, usually expressed as MUSTs, SHOULDs, HAVE TOs, GOT TOs, e.g. *I absolutely must not be rejected.* Unhealthy demands are not based on reality.

Rigid demands have three powerful unhealthy derivative beliefs:

1. **Awfulising** – an unrealistic assessment of *badness* where negative events are viewed or defined as 'end of the world bad' or 100% or more bad.
   Example: 'It would be awful if I'm rejected', 'It would be the end of the world if I am rejected and therefore I **must not** be rejected.'
2. **Low Frustration Tolerance (LFT)** – the *perceived* inability to tolerate frustration or difficulty even though we do tolerate it. We do not spontaneously combust and die in the face of frustration and difficulty.
   Example: 'Rejection is unbearable', 'I can't stand it', 'It's intolerable, therefore I **must not** be rejected.'
3. **Total Damning of Self or Other** – rating the self, another or the world in a totally negative way, based on a condition.
   Example: 'Rejection proves I'm a failure or worthless or unlovable as a person, therefore I **must not** be rejected.'

These beliefs are unhealthy because they generate emotional disturbance or unhealthy negative emotions like anxiety and depression. They are unrealistic, do not make sense and are unhelpful to you. They sabotage the achievement of your goals.

The Three Major MUSTs

Albert Ellis identified the unhealthy beliefs at the heart of most emotional problems. These can be placed under three major headings. Each of these core beliefs is based on rigid demands. They are as follows:

1. I *must* do well, greatly, perfectly, outstandingly and *must* win the approval of others *or else* it's awful, I can't stand it and I'm no good and I'll never do anything well. This can lead to many different types of unhealthy negative emotions like anxiety, depression, jealousy, hurt, unhealthy envy, guilt, shame and embarrassment and anger with the self.

2. Other people *must* do the right thing or be a certain way or treat me well or kindly and considerately and put me in the centre of their attention *or else* it's horrible, unbearable and proves they are bad and no good. This may lead to a variety of unhealthy negative emotions like anger, rage and jealousy, anxiety, depression and hurt.

3. Life *must* be easy, without discomfort or inconvenience or any hassle *or else* it's horrible, unbearable, that damned world doesn't give me everything with ease and without effort. This could lead to a number of unhealthy negative emotions like anxiety, anger and depression and a plethora of behavioural problems like avoidance, procrastination, addiction, giving up on goals to name but a few.

Think of the above three core beliefs as the roots of three different trees. Each tree will then have branches and many leaves on each branch. These branches and leaves represent the many different and specific examples of the core theme. You will find, like many people, that you may have specific issues stemming from all three core beliefs.

Healthy Beliefs

Beliefs that are healthy have, at their core, preferences, usually expressed as wants and desires. They are realistic, make sense and are helpful to you in the pursuit of your goals. Preference beliefs accept the reality of what **has** happened, what **is** happening and what **could** happen, whether we like it or not.

Preference beliefs are expressed by:

a. stating the desire
b. negation of the rigid demand.

For example: *'I'd prefer not to be rejected* **but** *it doesn't mean that I must not be.'* Preference beliefs lead to healthy negative emotions like concern and sadness as opposed to anxiety and depression. Anxiety and depression are provoked by unhealthy beliefs.

Preference beliefs have three powerful healthy derivative beliefs:

1. **Anti-awfulising** – negative events are placed on a scale of 0 – 99.9% badness where 100% bad does not exist, as one can usually think of something worse.
    Example: 'it would be bad but not the end of the world if I'm rejected.'
2. **High Frustration Tolerance (HFT)** – the realistic appraisal of your ability to tolerate frustration or difficulty.
    Example: 'If I'm rejected, it would be difficult but I can tolerate it.'
3. **Unconditional Acceptance of Self or Others** – unconditional acceptance of self, another or the world as fallible or imperfect. For example, acceptance of self is not dependent on conditions such as approval or love. You judge what you do rather than who or what you are (i.e. a complex human being).
    Example: 'I don't like the fact that I can be rejected but I accept myself unconditionally; I'm a fallible human being who will be rejected from time to time.'

Unhealthy beliefs (Demands, Awfulising, LFT and Total Damning) are rigid, inconsistent with reality, illogical and interfere with psychological well-being.

Healthy beliefs (Preferences, Anti-awfulising, HFT and Unconditional Acceptance) are flexible, consistent with reality, make sense and promote psychological well-being.

In summary:

Unhealthy Beliefs are:

RIGID
ILLOGICAL (don't make sense)
INCONSISTENT WITH REALITY
UNHELPFUL

Healthy Beliefs are:

FLEXIBLE
LOGICAL (make sense)
CONSISTENT WITH REALITY
HELPFUL

Negative Emotions

Unhealthy Negative Emotions v Healthy Negative Emotions

When we hold an unhealthy belief at **B** we disturb ourselves emotionally but when we hold a healthy belief at **B** we upset but **do not** disturb ourselves. Negative emotions can, therefore, be unhealthy or healthy depending on the view you take of the problem. The diagram below demonstrates this.

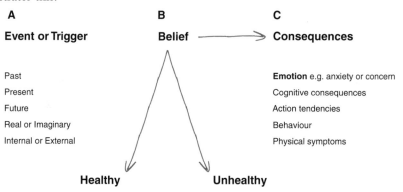

A	**B**	**C**
Event or Trigger	**Belief** ———⟶	**Consequences**

Past	**Emotion** e.g. anxiety or concern
Present	Cognitive consequences
Future	Action tendencies
Real or Imaginary	Behaviour
Internal or External	Physical symptoms

Healthy   **Unhealthy**

Example

A = your train is late
and you believe
B = 'The train MUST be on time; I can't stand it when the train is not on time'
then you will feel
C = Anger (unhealthy negative emotion)

On the other hand if you think healthily at

B = 'I'd like the train to be on time but it doesn't mean it absolutely MUST be on time; I can stand it being late even though I find it very frustrating'
then you're feeling at
C = Annoyance (healthy negative emotion)

Healthy negative emotions are transient because the underlying beliefs that provoke them are rational whereas unhealthy negative emotions are not and that is why changing the underlying belief to its healthy version releases you from being stuck emotionally.

There are eight unhealthy negative emotions and eight healthy counterparts. Below is a list, the left hand column giving you the general theme for each pair.

THEMES OF BELIEF	UNHEALTHY NEGATIVE EMOTIONS	HEALTHY NEGATIVE EMOTIONS
• Threat/Risk to You	• Anxiety	• Concern
• Your Loss/Failure	• Depression	• Sadness
• You are Treated Insensitively	• Hurt	• Sorrow/Disappointment
• You/Another Breaks Your Rule	• Anger	• Healthy Anger
• Threat to Your Relationship	• Jealousy	• Concern for Relationship
• Negative Revelation about You	• Shame/Embarrassment	• Regret
• You Break Your Moral Code	• Guilt	• Remorse
• Someone has Something You Want	• Unhealthy Envy	• Healthy Envy

Mixed Emotions

Often, when you have a problem you may have more than one emotion about that problem. For example, you may have experienced rejection and you may feel hurt, anxious and angry. You may feel hurt about being rejected, anxious about getting rejected again and angry about being rejected in a particular way. Each one of these emotions would be triggered by a distinct unhealthy belief.

Meta-emotions

You can create problems about problems. This means that you can have a secondary emotional problem about your primary emotional problem. The secondary emotion is called a meta-emotion or meta-problem. For example, you can feel depressed about your anxiety problem. Depression is the meta-emotion here.

Cognitive Consequences, Action Tendencies, Behaviours

When we experience an unhealthy negative emotion or a healthy negative emotion we:

a.   tend to think (cognitive consequences) in accordance with that emotional state, and

b.   feel like acting (action tendencies) in accordance with that emotional state.

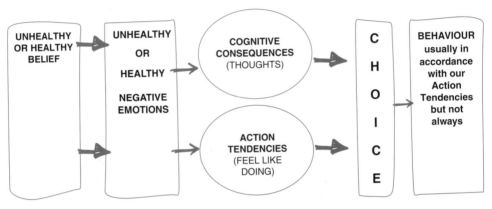

Beliefs, Cognitive Consequences, Action Tendencies and Behaviours

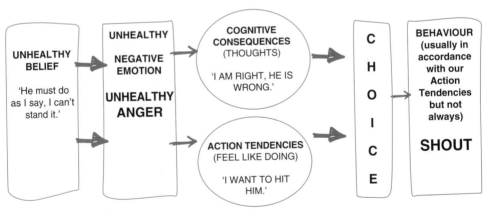

Example 1: Unhealthy Belief and its Consequences

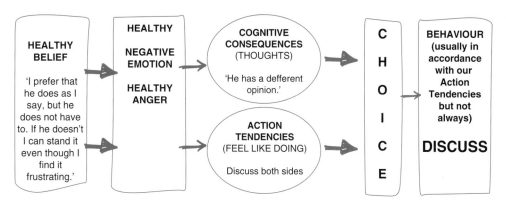

Example 2: Healthy Belief and its Consequences

As shown by the diagrams, the cognitive consequences of unhealthy negative emotions, due to holding unhealthy beliefs, are overly negative and unhelpful. The cognitive consequences of healthy negative emotions, due to holding healthy beliefs, are constructive and helpful.

In addition to beliefs affecting your thinking processes, they also influence the way in which you tend to act (action tendencies). If you hold unhealthy beliefs about something, your action tendencies will be self defeating. On the other hand, the action tendencies will be constructive if the beliefs held are healthy.

Whether you act on the tendency is a matter of choice. Just because you may have a tendency to act in a particular way does not mean that you will always behave in that way. You can choose to behave against what you feel like doing, i.e. **against** your unhelpful action tendencies. In order to overcome emotional problems you need to think in a healthy way and act in accordance with the helpful action tendencies.

Now that we have covered the basics of Emotional Responsibility, we'll explain how to use this book to help you to become more aware of your emotional state and how to take constructive action in order to move forward. The next section will explain how to use this book in detail.

How to Use This Book

This book is designed to be used in a number of different ways. You may use it to gain knowledge about emotional states and how we differentiate them in CBT or you may wish to use it for personal development, studies or to support your therapeutic work. The next eight chapters look at the eight unhealthy negative emotions and their healthy versions. The final chapter briefly explains the two main theories in CBT.

Each chapter contains an introduction to the title emotion and a checklist of triggers. A set of illustrations of both unhealthy and healthy cognitive consequences and action tendencies helps you identify the emotion. A guide for instigating emotional change then follows.

Each emotional pair is illustrated to show its cognitive consequences (how you think) and its action tendencies (what you feel like doing). You can compare and contrast the cognitive consequences and the action tendencies of anxiety and concern, for example. By looking at the illustrations and captions in each of the eight chapters on Emotions you can understand or become aware of your emotional state and whether it is healthy or unhealthy.

There are two ways of using this book if you wish to change your emotional state.

You may choose '**General Change**' or '**Philosophical Change**'.

General Change helps you work out for *yourself* how to modify your assumptions and behaviours by learning about the unhealthy and healthy negative emotions and their cognitive consequences and action tendencies. General Change does not deal with the underlying belief systems that provoke the cognitive consequences and action tendencies. If you wish to change the beliefs that trigger the cognitive consequences and action tendencies, then you should choose the philosophical route and learn how to do that.

Philosophical Change is a more directive approach focusing you on identifying your unhealthy beliefs. It teaches you how to dispute them, work out their healthy counterparts and dispute them too. Disputing is a key skill in Philosophical Change. Disputing involves questioning the reality, sense and helpfulness of your beliefs.

This is done in order to help you understand the healthy solution to solving the problem. You will see, from the example later on in this chapter, the disputation questions to ask. Finally, Philosophical Change involves implementing the healthy solutions to your problem by thinking and acting in accordance with your healthy beliefs.

General Change helps you to manage your emotions and symptoms whereas Philosophical Change helps you to get better in the long term. It enables you to face what you are most disturbing yourself about and then develop a healthy rational response to it. You learn a philosophy that you can then generalise to other areas of your life. Below are two examples that demonstrate the difference between General Change and Philosophical Change.

Example 1: Dealing with the problem of rejection.
In General Change, you will realistically understand that you might not get rejected. You will focus on the likelihood of getting rejected and work out that, in reality, you may or may not get rejected.

Philosophical Change starts by pushing the button – it assumes rejection will happen to you and then helps you work out the unhealthy belief you hold about being rejected. It focuses you on facing the possibility of rejection rather than focusing you on the likelihood of rejection.

Example 2: Dealing with anxiety about dying in an aeroplane incident.
In General Change you will realise that flying is a safe mode of transport, disasters are rare and that the odds are stacked strongly in your favour. The likelihood of arriving safely at your destination is almost, but not quite, certain.

With Philosophical Change you will face the reality that risk exists, no matter how improbable. It helps you accept and develop a healthy attitude to adverse possibilities and uncertainty.

If you choose General Change but find yourself thinking 'Yes, but?' then the Philosophical Change method is for you.

We prefer Philosophical Change because it focuses on the most disturbing aspect of any problem first.

General Change has five steps

STEP 1   Choose a typical example of your emotional problem.

STEP 2   Identify your cognitive consequences and action tendencies that relate to your unhealthy negative emotion. Write them in your own words, using the illustrations as a guide. Make sure that they are specific to your example.

STEP 3   Repeat the above, this time identifying your cognitive consequences and action tendencies that relate to the healthy negative emotion.

STEP 4   Commit to thinking and behaving in accordance with the cognitive consequences and action tendencies of the healthy negative emotion.

STEP 5   Repeat, Repeat, Repeat in a consistent and forceful manner until your new thinking and your new behaviour become second nature.

Example of General Change – Presentation Anxiety

1   You have identified that you feel anxious about doing a presentation.

2   One of the cognitive consequences of anxiety is *'You create an even more negative threat in your mind'*, so you might write, *'I think the presentation will go badly and I will end up losing my job'*. One of the action tendencies of anxiety is *'You seek reassurance'* so you might write, *'I keep wanting to ask and ask my colleagues to tell me that all will be fine.'*

3   Now look at the cognitive consequences and action tendencies for the healthy negative emotion of concern. One of the cognitive consequences of concern is *'You do not create an even more negative threat in your mind.'* You might write, *'I hope all will be fine and it's unlikely that I will lose my job if it doesn't go well.'*
    One of the action tendencies of concern is to *'Deal with the threat constructively.'* So you might write, *'I will not seek constant reassurance.'*

4   Commit to thinking and behaving in accordance with the cognitive consequences and action tendencies of the healthy negative emotion.

5   Repeat, Repeat, Repeat in a consistent and forceful manner until your new thinking and your new behaviour become second nature.

Having followed through to the last step, you should begin to think healthy thoughts when you think about your presentation and you should stop yourself from seeking reassurance.

Philosophical Change has five steps

STEP 1 **Identify your unhealthy belief by:**
  a. Choosing a typical example of your emotional problem.
  b. Using the Common (Emotion) Triggers table as a reference to pinpoint what you are feeling most disturbed about.
  c. Express your answer to (b) in the form of a 'MUST'.
  d. Identify the three derivative beliefs. (Awfulising, Low Frustration Tolerance and Damning). You may have all three derivatives or any combination of the three. You should imagine yourself in the trigger situation when identifying the derivative beliefs.

STEP 2 **Dispute your unhealthy belief.**
  The unhealthy belief is made up of the rigid demand and its derivatives. The disputing questions below are used on all of them.
  a. Are they realistic or not and why?
  b. Do they make sense or not and why?
  c. Do they lead to helpful or unhelpful outcomes for me, and why?

STEP 3 **Identify your healthy belief.**
  This is done by rewriting the unhealthy belief into its healthy version. The healthy version of the rigid demand is called a preference belief. Three balanced beliefs are derived from the preference belief. (Anti-awfulising, High Frustration Tolerance and Unconditional Acceptance of Self or Other.)

STEP 4 **Dispute your healthy belief.**
  The healthy belief is made up of the preference belief and its derivatives. The disputing questions below are used on all of them.
  a. Are they realistic or not and why?
  b. Do they make sense or not and why?
  c. Do they lead to helpful or unhelpful outcomes for me, and why?

STEP 5 **Strengthen your healthy belief and weaken your unhealthy belief.**
  A number of cognitive and behavioural assignments are suggested in each chapter.

Example of Philosophical Change – Presentation Anxiety

1   You have identified the following belief that triggers Presentation Anxiety: My colleagues **must** not judge me negatively if I appear nervous. It would:
    * be **awful** if they did.
    * be **unbearable** if they did.
    * prove **I'm worthless** if they did.

2   The unhealthy beliefs (Rigid demand, Awfulising, Low Frustration Tolerance) are each disputed by asking the following:
    a.   Are they realistic or not and why?
    b.   Do they make sense or not and why?
    c.   Do they lead to helpful or unhelpful outcomes for me, and why?

3   Identify the healthy belief. The unhealthy belief is rewritten into its healthy version below:
    I'd prefer that my colleagues did not judge me negatively if I appear nervous but that does not mean that it absolutely **must** not happen. If they judged me negatively it would:
    * be bad but **not awful.**
    * be difficult but **not unbearable.**
    * **not mean that I am worthless.** I am a fallible human being and my worth does not depend on whether my colleagues judge me negatively or not.

4   The healthy belief is disputed by asking the following questions about the preference belief and its derivatives:
    a.   Are they realistic or not and why?
    b.   Do they make sense or not and why?
    c.   Do they lead to helpful or unhelpful outcomes for me, and why?

5   Strengthen your healthy belief and weaken your unhealthy belief, by reciting the healthy belief whilst imagining yourself looking nervous in front of your colleagues. Also, behave in accordance with healthy action tendencies such as not seeking reassurance and not avoiding presentations.

We believe that making a philosophical shift is a more effective way of getting better in the long term because you will be working on the auto pilot that provokes your unhealthy emotions, thoughts and tendencies to behave, i.e. your beliefs.

You will be able to generalise what you have learnt to other areas of your life too, as you will have learnt a philosophy for healthy living.

Whichever route of change you choose – General or Philosophical Change – you will enable yourself to make helpful positive changes to your well-being. Beginning to recognise how your thoughts impact on your life experience is empowering.

Choosing General Change will enable you to figure out for yourself how you need to think and what you need to do to manage your emotions more healthily.

Philosophical Change takes more time and focus and will enable you to change underlying unhealthy beliefs to more healthy counterparts. On achieving this specific change you can then go on to generalise this healthy way of thinking and apply it to other areas in your life.

However you choose to use this book, we hope that you find it helpful.

Humour

We have used humour in some of the illustrations to help you remember some of the points and also because we believe in taking things seriously but not too seriously. Indeed, psychological health has been summarised by this philosophy by many great thinkers. But remember to put the emphasis on not taking things *too* seriously. It shouldn't be interpreted as 'it doesn't matter to me'.

Using humour is about demonstrating how unhealthy and irrational our thoughts and behaviours can be. It is not about poking fun at anyone. No one is perfect and a key aspect of CBT is about accepting ourselves unconditionally as fallible human beings who can at times think and act in unhealthy ways. Accepting this fact helps us to move forward.

Illustration Conventions

We have used the standard illustration conventions for this book.

Cognitive consequences are illustrated using 'thought' bubbles.

Action tendencies are illustrated, where relevant, with 'speech' bubbles.

The original inspiration for the illustrated figures came from two boys from a little village called Samode, Rajastan, India. At the time, Patrick (the illustrator) was sketching a street view of the village. Patrick says:

These two young boys, one about 8 and the other perhaps 10 or 11, were curious about me. Their faces showed (I thought) rather conflicting emotions. On one side, friendly curiosity and on the other, disapproval: 'What was this foreigner doing on our patch?'

This was fairly rural India and I don't suppose they saw many Westerners. I thought that this image of these two boys might just fit with the premise of this book, that one's emotions can lead one in different directions, healthy or unhealthy. My original intention was to have the boys in every illustration but it became rapidly clear that such a concept would be nigh on impossible to continue over such a broad swathe of emotions. However, they do appear here and there and they have been my starting point for many of the images. These boys will be young men now . . .

A Final Note Before You Get Started

This book has been written to help you gain insight about emotions and understand how to change the unhealthy negative ones by working on the unhealthy beliefs that provoke them. We recommend professional intervention if your emotional state is so overwhelming that working on them on your own proves to be too much for you. You will find additional information for seeking professional help at the end of the book.

CHAPTER 1

Anxiety and Concern

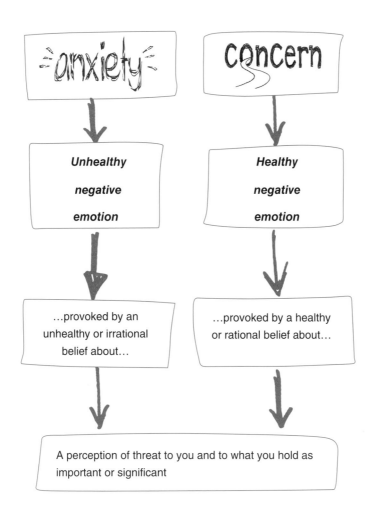

W e will focus on the most common forms of anxieties that we see in our private practice.

Anxiety

You can be anxious about a number of things at the same time. For example:

- Being judged negatively
- Anxiety itself
- Not achieving your personal goal
- Failure
- Something happening or not happening.

It is important to understand whether these different anxieties are dependent or independent of each other.

A person might be worried that if they do not perform well they will be judged negatively, and if this was to happen it would mean they are worthless. These two anxieties are therefore dependent on each other; performing well may be hiding the deeper anxiety about negative judgement. In effect, the person is saying that if the possibility of negative judgement didn't exist then they wouldn't be anxious about their performance. The main focus of their anxiety is negative judgement and performing well is a strategy designed to avoid negative judgement. In this case the problem is created by an unhealthy belief about negative judgement, i.e. I MUST not be judged negatively and in order for that not to happen I MUST perform well.

Other people may have anxiety about negative judgement and also anxiety about their performance but independently of one another. In other words the anxiety about negative judgement and the anxiety about their performance are mutually exclusive and are two distinct events. In this case there are two independent unhealthy beliefs; one about negative judgement and the other about performance, i.e. I MUST not be judged negatively and I MUST perform according to my expectation. If you asked this person to imagine that people would not judge them negatively regardless of how badly they performed, would they still be anxious about their performance? If they said 'yes, I would because I really want to do well for me too', then the two anxieties are *not* dependent on each other.

If you are anxious about more than one thing, reflect on whether these anxieties are dependent or independent. This will then help you to work out the unhealthy belief or beliefs that are relevant as you work through the chapter.

Anxiety about Anxiety

A common form of anxiety is anxiety about anxiety, i.e. fear of the fear. When you experience anxiety a number of things happen. You clearly feel the emotion of anxiety but you also experience thoughts as well as physical sensations. It is important to ask yourself 'why is the emotion of anxiety so problematic for me? What do I become worried about when I experience anxiety?' The following are some common reasons for being anxious about anxiety.

- **Fear of negative judgement about looking anxious** – they fear others will notice they are anxious or because they might forget what they were saying, tremble, blush or sweat, and that others will negatively judge them for being so.
- **Fear of the physical symptoms of anxiety** – in a state of anxiety they become aware of their heart beat rising and they worry they might have a heart attack, or they get uncomfortable physical symptoms and pains like dizziness, nausea, headaches, migraines, irritable bowel, losing control of their bowels and so forth, which trigger the anxiety response.
- **Fear of the mental symptoms of anxiety** – in a state of anxiety their thoughts become jumbled up and they worry that if they can't control their thoughts they will lose their mind.
- **Fear of anxiety attacks** – this is known as Panic Disorder. Some people are anxious about being anxious because they worry that in a state of anxiety they might have a panic attack. They may worry that having a panic attack could lead to a heart attack, death, losing control of their mind, losing control of themselves in front of others or some other negative event they view as awful, unbearable or a threat to their self esteem.

Anxiety about Uncertainty

Another common form of anxiety is about uncertainty, although this does not appear to stand alone. We have not encountered any clients who present for therapy complaining about being anxious about uncertainty. What we have encountered are people who are aware of specific threats and risks and demand certainty about them. For example, some people become anxious about physical health and then demand certainty that they are safe from such a risk. They will usually check the internet, regularly seek medical tests and are in a constant state of anxiety because their most cherished desire is certainty that no harm will come to them. Obsessive Compulsive Disorder is essentially about attempting to eliminate risk and sufferers demand certainty and a complete absence of doubt about possible adversities such as contamination, safety and security. Not knowing is therefore extremely uncomfortable. Anxiety about uncertainty can be linked to the threat of making mistakes, making the wrong decisions or not knowing whether something has happened or not.

Generally speaking it is triggered by rigid beliefs and low frustration tolerance beliefs. For example, I MUST be sure that my decision is right, not knowing for sure is intolerable, or I MUST be certain I won't have depression again and so forth.

Common Anxiety Triggers

The following are common triggers of anxiety – the list is not exhaustive. Some anxieties may be formed around a specific core theme such as perfectionism, control or comfort. Tick the boxes that you think apply to you.

Tick the box to identify your anxiety triggers

- ☐ Failure
- ☐ Success
- ☐ Making mistakes
- ☐ Negative judgement by others
- ☐ Approval
- ☐ Not being loved
- ☐ Rejection
- ☐ Loneliness
- ☐ Decision making
- ☐ Blushing
- ☐ Sweating
- ☐ Safety
- ☐ Loss of control
- ☐ Loss of order
- ☐ Certainty

- ☐ Anxiety itself
- ☐ Not knowing
- ☐ Heart attack
- ☐ Negative emotions
- ☐ Effort
- ☐ Health
- ☐ Not having positive emotions
- ☐ Images or thoughts both judged as shocking or reprehensible
- ☐ Boredom
- ☐ Illness
- ☐ Physical symptoms and sensations such as dizziness or nausea
- ☐ Loss of bodily functions, i.e. incontinence in public

☐ Death

☐ Others feeling angry with you

☐ Financial

☐ Others not meeting your
expectations

☐ Others feeling hurt or upset about
something you said or did

☐ Specific thoughts

☐ Confrontation

☐ Losing your mind

☐ Other (write your own reason)

Am I Anxious or Concerned?

At the heart of your anxiety are unhealthy beliefs about either a perceived or a real threat or danger to you or to what matters to you. The things that matter to you are usually your family, friends, relationships, finance, to name but a few.

Perceived threat is different from real threat in that the threat does not exist in physical reality. It is created by our images and thoughts about a person or situation. For example, anxiety about spiders can happen when a person perceives the small house spider as very large or dangerous when in reality it is a house spider. When we are faced with perceived or real threats, what we believe will determine the level of unhealthy anxiety or healthy concern we feel.

Unhealthy beliefs not only provoke anxiety but they have a consequence on how you think (cognitive consequences), act or tend to act (action tendencies). When you feel anxious, for example, your thoughts may be preoccupied with 'what if' and you may avoid or seek constant assurance and reassurance.

Assess if you are anxious or concerned by checking your cognitive consequences and action tendencies.

Look through the illustrations for the cognitive consequences and action tendencies and work out if you are anxious or concerned. It is important to put yourself in the trigger situation when you felt nervous. It is easy to think that you don't have unhealthy beliefs and thoughts when you are not triggered or when you are away from the threat. Imagine yourself in the frying pan, so to speak, then work out if the nervousness was anxiety or concern.

Anxiety

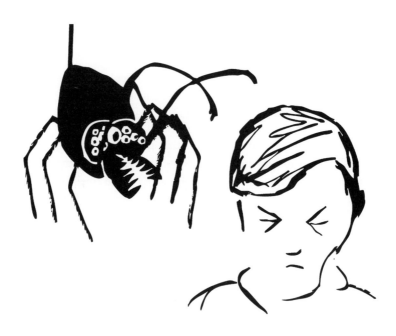

You tend to overestimate negative features of the threat.

Cognitive Consequences

Concern

You view the threat realistically.

Cognitive Consequences

Anxiety

You underestimate ability to cope with the threat.

Cognitive Consequences

Concern

You realistically appraise your ability to cope with threat.

Anxiety

You create an even more negative threat in your mind.

Cognitive Consequences

Concern

You do not create an even more negative threat in your mind.

Cognitive Consequences

Anxiety

You have more task irrelevant thoughts than in concern.

Cognitive Consequences

Concern

You have more task relevant thoughts than in anxiety.

You withdraw physically from the threat.

You face up to the threat.

Action/Action Tendencies

Anxiety

You withdraw mentally from the threat.

Action/Action Tendencies

Concern

You deal with the threat constructively.

Action/Action Tendencies

Anxiety

garlic

crucifix

salt

dark glasses

black cat

worry beads

copper band

hand of glory

towel

shrunken head

tincture of recovery

invisibility scarf

'An Armoury of Wards'

You ward off the threat, e.g. with superstition.

Action/Action Tendencies

Concern

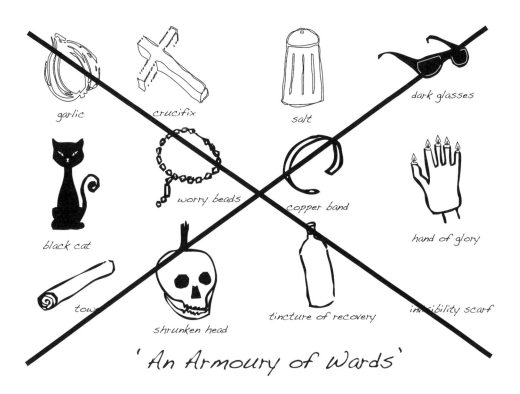

garlic

crucifix

salt

dark glasses

black cat

worry beads

copper band

hand of glory

tow...

shrunken head

tincture of recovery

invisibility scarf

'An Armoury of Wards'

You do not ward off the threat, e.g. you have no superstitions.

Anxiety

You tranquillise your feelings.

Action/Action Tendencies

Concern

You accept and allow your feelings.

You seek reassurance.

Concern

You do not seek reassurance.

Now . . .

General Change or Philosophical Change for you?

General Change

STEP 1   Choose a typical example of your anxiety problem.

STEP 2   Identify your anxiety cognitive consequences and action tendencies and write them in your own words, using the illustrations as a guide. Make sure that they are specific to your example.

STEP 3   Identify your concern cognitive consequences and action tendencies and write them in your own words, using the illustrations as a guide. Make sure they are specific to your example.

STEP 4   Commit to thinking and behaving in accordance with your healthy cognitive consequences and action tendencies for concern.

STEP 5   Repeat, Repeat, Repeat in a consistent and forceful manner until your new thinking and your new behaviour become second nature.

> **Tip:**
> If behaving in accordance with healthy concern is too overwhelming to begin with, then *imagine* yourself behaving in a healthy manner for a few weeks and then start in real life.

Philosophical Change

Remember to take your time if you are choosing this route, as Philosophical Change is about changing your unhealthy beliefs over the long term.

STEP 1   Identify your unhealthy belief.

STEP 2   Dispute your unhealthy belief.

STEP 3   Identify your healthy belief.

STEP 4   Dispute your healthy belief.

STEP 5   Strengthen your healthy belief and weaken your unhealthy belief.

Remember, anxiety is provoked by unhealthy beliefs about perceived or real threats. An unhealthy belief is made up of absolutist **rigid beliefs** in the form of a MUST, HAVE TO, NEED TO, GOT TO, ABSOLUTELY SHOULD, from which three further derivative disturbed beliefs come.

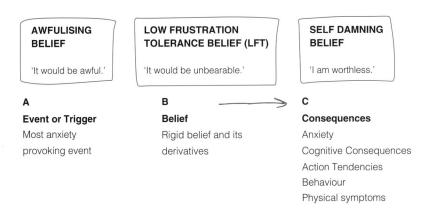

A   B   ⟶   C

Event or Trigger   **Belief**   **Consequences**

Most anxiety   Rigid belief and its   Anxiety

provoking event   derivatives   Cognitive Consequences

                                                Action Tendencies

                                                Behaviour

                                                Physical symptoms

A rigid unhealthy belief, at **B**, is a demand about the most anxiety provoking aspect of an event – it is either a demand for it to **absolutely happen** or **absolutely not happen**.

For example, if what you are most anxious about is success, then the rigid belief is **I must succeed**. If what you are most anxious about is failing, then the rigid belief is **I must not fail**. The consequence of not having the rigid belief met are any, a combination of, or all of the three derivative beliefs.

For example:

RIGID BELIEF	AWFULISING BELIEF	LOW FRUSTRATION TOLERANCE BELIEF	SELF DAMNING BELIEF
'I MUST not fail because …'	'…failure would be awful'	'…and failure would be unbearable'	'…and if I fail it would prove I am a failure.'

Step 1

Identify your unhealthy anxiety provoking belief

a. Choose a typical example of your anxiety problem.

b. Use the previous Common Anxiety Triggers table as a reference to pinpoint what you were *most* anxious about. You may have more than one trigger, which means you may have more than one anxiety provoking belief. Work on one belief at a time.

c. Express your answer to Question (b) above in the form of a 'MUST'. (See previous examples.)

d. Identify the three derivative beliefs. (Awfulising, Low Frustration Tolerance (LFT), Self Damning. See page 5 as a reminder to what these mean.)

You may have all three derivatives or any combination of the three.

Remember to imagine yourself in the trigger situation when identifying these derivative beliefs.

Examples	A	LFT	SD/OD
'I must not be rejected; getting rejected would be awful, unbearable and prove I'm worthless.'	✓	✓	✓
'I must be in control of my body; not being in control is unbearable.'		✓	
'I must be certain my decision is correct; not knowing is awful and I cannot bear it.'	✓	✓	
'I must not get a migraine when I'm anxious; a migraine is awful and intolerable.'	✓	✓	
'People must think in a positive way about me; if they don't it means I'm a failure.'			✓

Key: A = Awfulising, LFT = Low Frustration Tolerance, SD = Self Damning, OD = Other Damning

Step 2

dispute? your unhealthy anxiety provoking belief

Question the validity of your unhealthy belief, using the following three criteria. Remember that an unhealthy belief is made up of the rigid belief and its derivatives. The disputing questions below are used on all of them.

a. Are they realistic or not and why?
b. Do they make sense or not and why?
c. Do they lead to helpful or unhelpful outcomes for me, and why?

Let's assume your unhealthy belief was as follows:

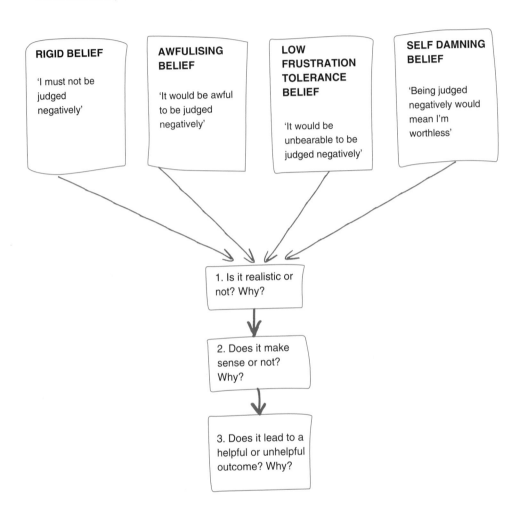

RIGID BELIEF

'I must not be judged negatively'

AWFULISING BELIEF

'It would be awful to be judged negatively'

LOW FRUSTRATION TOLERANCE BELIEF

'It would be unbearable to be judged negatively'

SELF DAMNING BELIEF

'Being judged negatively would mean I'm worthless'

1. Is it realistic or not? Why?

2. Does it make sense or not? Why?

3. Does it lead to a helpful or unhelpful outcome? Why?

Go ahead and dispute your unhealthy belief or beliefs.

Step 3

Identify your healthy concern provoking belief

a. Change your unhealthy belief and work out the healthy version by removing the rigidity and replacing it with the preference belief.

b. Remember to negate your unhealthy demand. For example, 'I want to be judged in a positive way but I absolutely don't have to be'.

c. Identify the derivative beliefs. (Anti-awfulising, High Frustration Tolerance (HFT), Self/Other/World Acceptance. See page 7 as a reminder to what these mean.) Use the examples below as a guide.

d. Remember, preference beliefs are flexible, make sense and lead to a helpful outcome.

Unhealthy beliefs	A	LFT	SD/OD
'I must not be rejected; getting rejected would be awful, unbearable and prove I'm worthless.'	✓	✓	✓
'I must be in control of my body; not being in control is unbearable.'		✓	
'I must be certain my decision is correct; not knowing is awful and I cannot bear it.'	✓	✓	
'I must not get a migraine when I'm anxious; a migraine is awful and intolerable.'	✓	✓	
'People must think in a positive way about me; if they don't it means I'm a failure.'			✓

Healthy versions	AA	HFT	SA/OA
'I would prefer to be accepted and not rejected but it doesn't mean that I absolutely must. If I'm rejected it would be bad but not awful, difficult but not unbearable and it would not mean I'm worthless. I accept myself regardless.'	✓	✓	✓
'I would like to be in control of my body but it does not mean I absolutely must. If I'm not it would be difficult but not unbearable.'		✓	
'I'd like to be certain my decision is correct but it doesn't mean that I absolutely must be. Not being certain is bad but not the end of the world, difficult and frustrating but I can bear it.'	✓	✓	
'I'd rather I didn't get a migraine when I get anxious but it doesn't mean that I musn't. A migraine is difficult and painful but I cope and tolerate it. A migraine is really bad but not the end of the world, it is difficult and painful but I cope and tolerate it.'	✓	✓	
'I'd like people to think of me in a positive way but they don't have to. If they don't it doesn't mean I'm a failure. I accept myself regardless. I'm fallible.'			✓

Key: A = Awfulising, LFT = Low Frustration Tolerance, SD = Self Damning, OD = Other Damning, AA = Anti Awfulising, HFT = High Frustration Tolerance, SA = Self Acceptance, OA = Other Acceptance

Go ahead and rewrite your beliefs in a healthy way.

Step 4

dispute? your healthy concern provoking belief

Dispute your healthy beliefs using the same criteria used in disputing the unhealthy beliefs – this keeps it fair and you are more likely to persuade yourself to commit to changing them if you dispute the unhealthy and the healthy beliefs in exactly the same way.

Remember that a healthy belief is made up of a preference belief and its three balanced derivatives or a combination of them. The disputing questions below are used on all of them.

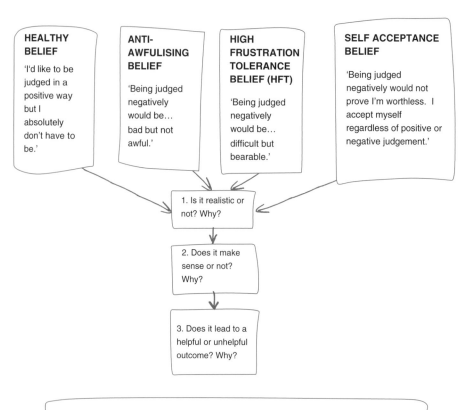

HEALTHY BELIEF

'I'd like to be judged in a positive way but I absolutely don't have to be.'

ANTI-AWFULISING BELIEF

'Being judged negatively would be… bad but not awful.'

HIGH FRUSTRATION TOLERANCE BELIEF (HFT)

'Being judged negatively would be… difficult but bearable.'

SELF ACCEPTANCE BELIEF

'Being judged negatively would not prove I'm worthless. I accept myself regardless of positive or negative judgement.'

1. Is it realistic or not? Why?

2. Does it make sense or not? Why?

3. Does it lead to a helpful or unhelpful outcome? Why?

Tip:
Remember that anti-awfulising is where 100% bad does not exist, as one can usually think of something worse.

Tip:
HFT means you have not disintegrated.

Tip:
Self/other acceptance is not based on conditions. We are all fallible human beings.

Go ahead and dispute your healthy belief and its balanced derivatives.

Step 5

STRENGTHEN your healthy concern provoking belief

weaken your unhealthy anxiety provoking belief

In order to change your anxiety provoking belief to a healthy concern provoking one, you should think in accordance with your healthy belief and take constructive actions. The illustrations demonstrate the thinking (cognitive consequences) and action tendencies of concern. The constructive actions are based on the action tendencies of concern.

- Think and act in accordance with your healthy belief repeatedly and consistently in a forceful manner until eventually your emotional state changes from anxiety to a healthier one of concern.

- Remember your emotion of anxiety **will** change – the new way of thinking and the new actions you will implement will feel uncomfortable initially but this is completely natural. You are changing an old habit of unhealthy thinking and old habitual anxiety behaviours. It takes a few weeks of repetitions done consistently and forcefully.

- The behavioural goals you set for yourself need to be challenging but not overwhelming. If you overwhelm yourself then it defeats the object of the exercise.

- Start with imagining yourself thinking and acting in a healthy manner using your healthy belief whilst being in the trigger situation until you think you are ready to challenge yourself in real life. For example, imagining yourself going to the gym is a good start but at some point you will need to take action and go to the gym and then continue until you achieve your desired goal.

- Repeat your healthy belief of concern in your head daily and particularly when you are imagining yourself in the trigger situation. This mental rehearsal will help you to remember it when you deliberately face the trigger situation in real life.

- Once you achieve your desired goal, whatever it is, then you need to maintain the helpful thinking and actions. For example, if you achieve your target weight from going to the gym, it would be unwise to stop completely.

- Review how you did, each time you challenge yourself, and then work out what you can do differently or better the next time. Then do it. Do not demand perfection from yourself. The process of moving from anxiety to concern is uncomfortable and uneven. Some days you will make bigger strides when you challenge yourself and other days you will make small strides or even take a step back. The important thing is to accept that this can happen and then bring your focus back to what you are doing and continue with it.

- Remember, you didn't learn to drive a car, ride a bicycle or learn to read overnight, it takes repetition and focus and consistency.

Chapter 1 – Anxiety – Takeaway Tips

- To overcome anxiety, it is vital that any avoidance is eliminated. We tend to avoid thoughts, behaviours, feelings, physical sensations, mental images, situations, objects, animals and people. Recite your healthy belief in your head whenever you are feeling like you wish to avoid your particular anxiety provoking situations.

- Learn relaxation techniques but ensure that you are not using relaxation to avoid the feeling of anxiety. Learn relaxation to have a balance in your life.

- Exercise regularly but make sure that you are not using exercising as a strategy to avoid the feeling of anxiety. Exercise to have a healthy lifestyle.

- Challenge yourself but do not overwhelm yourself.

- Face your anxiety triggers bit by bit.

- Repeat, repeat and repeat and be consistent.

CHAPTER 2

Depression and Sadness

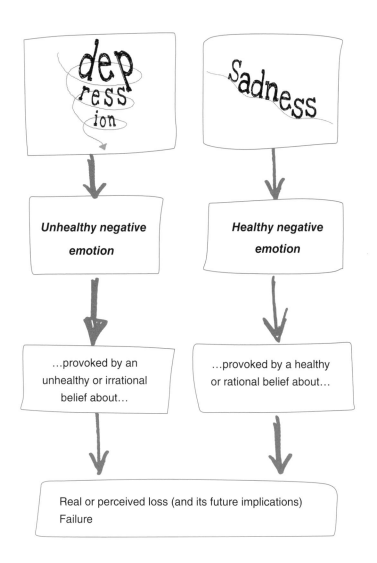

Depression is second to anxiety as the most commonly experienced emotional disturbance.

Depression can affect us all at some point or another; women have over twice the incidence of depression than men. This is thought to be due to hormonal influences throughout a woman's life.

Here we will explore psychologically based depression as opposed to chemically or organically based depression.

Types of Depression

There are several different types of depression. They are usually distinguished by their dominant features, duration and severity of symptoms. Most of these kinds of depression are defined by the *Diagnostic and Statistical Manual of Mental Disorders* (DSM), an American Psychiatric Association publication.

The following three different kinds of depression are distinct depressive disorders described in the DSM. Sufferers experience significant distress and /or impairment of functioning, e.g. work, school, relationships and so on.

Major Depressive Disorder (also known as Major Depression, Clinical Depression) – A major depressive episode occurs with symptoms that last for most of the day, nearly every day for at least two weeks.

Dysthymic Disorder – This is less severe than Major Depression but lasts at least two years.

Bipolar Affective Disorder – also known as Manic Depression or Bipolar Disorder. This is a condition which causes mood swings. Your mood varies from excitement to depression and despair. You may also have hallucinations.

Other types of depression include:

Seasonal Affective Disorder (SAD) – This is a type of depression with a seasonal pattern, occurring most commonly in the winter months.

Postnatal Depression – This develops two to three weeks after childbirth and lasts for months or even years.

Chronic Depression – This is a Major depressive episode that lasts for at least two years.

Endogenous Depression – This type of depression is defined as feeling depressed for no apparent reason.

Reactive Depression – Depression is felt after experiencing a specific stressor such as loss or failure. The depression occurs within three months and lasts no longer than six months.

You can be depressed in a variety of different ways.

We can all experience depression because loss and failure are part of life. Whether we do or don't is largely due to our beliefs, which can be healthy or unhealthy. Sadness is the healthy counterpart of debilitating depression.

Paul Hauck, an American psychologist, has observed that you can depress yourself in three ways:

1. Self denigration
2. Self pity
3. Other pity

Self denigration depression is triggered by holding rigid beliefs about autonomy, independence, success and freedom.

For example:

- I absolutely should be able to look after myself.
- I absolutely have to be independent.
- I should always succeed; the fact that I am not succeeding proves I am a total failure and worthless.

Self damning or denigration beliefs may also be related to holding rigid beliefs about acceptance or rejection by someone significant or by your community. For example, '*I should not have been rejected. The fact that I have been proves I am bad, worthless*', and so on.

Self pity depression is based on thinking 'Why Me?', 'Poor me', 'I don't deserve this'. Self pity depression usually occurs after a loss such as losing a loved one, job or relationship. It is triggered by holding unhealthy demands that life must be comfortable, easy and hassle free.

Other pity depression occurs when you disturb yourself about people's plight, pain and suffering and misfortune, creating demands such as *'Injustice absolutely should not happen. People must not suffer so badly, it's awful that they do.'*

Anxiety about Depression

You can experience anxiety about becoming depressed or about remaining depressed forever.

You might think 'I must never be depressed again; I couldn't stand it. I must know for sure I will never be depressed again.' This unhealthy belief will lead to anxiety about depression as well as unhelpful behaviours such as seeking constant reassurance.

The aim should be to experience concern about the future possibility of depression rather than anxiety.

Unhealthy Anger about Depression

If you hold a belief that depression is a sign of weakness then it is quite likely that you will feel unhealthy anger towards yourself for being depressed. Unhealthy anger is provoked by unhealthy beliefs about frustration or breaking of a personal rule.

For example, you may demand very high standards of performance from yourself at work. When you fail to meet those demands you can become depressed because you believe *'I am a total failure.'* You can then feel angry with yourself for becoming depressed.

This unhealthy anger is triggered by holding an unhealthy belief about depression, e.g. *'I should not be feeling depression as it proves I am weak'*, leading to self defeating behaviours such as over drinking or shouting at others.

Guilt about Depression

If you hold an unhealthy belief that '*I shouldn't be depressed, it's wrong as I have so much in my life to be grateful for*', you will feel guilt about the feeling of depression. At the heart of guilt is an unhealthy belief that '*I should be grateful for what I've got. The fact that I am not means I am a bad person.*'

Shame about Depression

Often when we are depressed we may hold a belief that 'I shouldn't be feeling depressed' or reveal to others that we are depressed, for example, 'If others know I'm depressed they will judge me as weak and I agree with them because depression is a sign of weakness.' You may then pretend all is well or you may isolate yourself further to save face.

Feeling shame about depression or shame about having emotional problems is, unfortunately, very common.

Common Depression Triggers

The following are common triggers of depression – the list is not exhaustive. Depression is provoked by having an unhealthy belief about loss or failure. Tick the boxes that you think apply to you.

Tick the box to identify your depression triggers

☐ Failure
☐ Goals blocked
☐ Loss of status
☐ Loss of autonomy
☐ Inability to do prized activities (disabilities)
☐ Being dependent on others
☐ Loss of choice
☐ Loss of self control
☐ Loss of approval
☐ Rejection
☐ Criticism/Disapproval
☐ Loss of love
☐ Negative evaluation from others
☐ Losing connection with significant others
☐ Being on one's own
☐ Loss of reputation or social standing
☐ Loss of helping role
☐ Hardship
☐ Others' misfortune
☐ Others withdrawing support
☐ Boredom
☐ Loss of health/Illness/Heart attack

☐ Unattractiveness
☐ Unfairness
☐ Bereavement/Death
☐ Not having positive emotions
☐ Others feeling angry with you
☐ Financial
☐ Specific thoughts
☐ Not belonging
☐ Failure to keep control
☐ Limited choice
☐ Other (write your own reason)

Am I Depressed or Sad?

At the heart of depression are unhealthy beliefs about real or perceived loss or failure.

Such unhealthy beliefs not only provoke depression but they have a consequence on how you think (cognitive consequences) and how you feel like behaving (action tendencies).

When you feel depressed, for example, your thoughts may be preoccupied with 'if only' and you may avoid friends and family and try to withdraw from the world.

Assess if you are depressed or sad by checking your cognitive consequences and action tendencies.

Look through the illustrations for the cognitive consequences and action tendencies and work out if you are depressed or sad. It is important to put yourself in the trigger situation.

It is easy to think that you don't have unhealthy beliefs and thoughts when you are not triggered or when you are away from the problem. Imagine yourself in the situation that triggered your low mood and then work out if the emotion was depression or sadness.

Cognitive Consequences

Depression

You only see the negative aspects of the loss or failure.

Cognitive Consequences

Sadness

You can see both negative and positive aspects of the loss or failure.

Cognitive Consequences

Depression

You think of other losses and failures that you have experienced.

Cognitive Consequences

Sadness

You are less likely to think of other losses and failures than when you are depressed.

Cognitive Consequences

Depression

You think you are unable to help yourself (helplessness).

Cognitive Consequences

Sadness

You are able to help yourself.

Depression

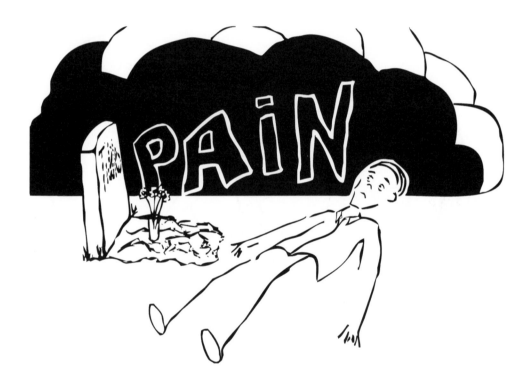

You only see pain and blackness in the future (hopelessness).

Cognitive Consequences

Sadness

You can see the future with hope.

Depression

You withdraw from reinforcements.

Action/Action Tendencies

Sadness

You are able to express your feelings about the loss or failure and talk to significant others.

Depression

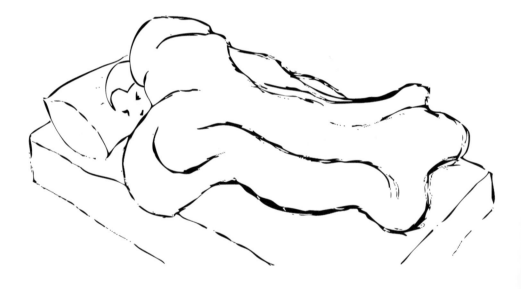

You withdraw into yourself.

Action/Action Tendencies

Sadness

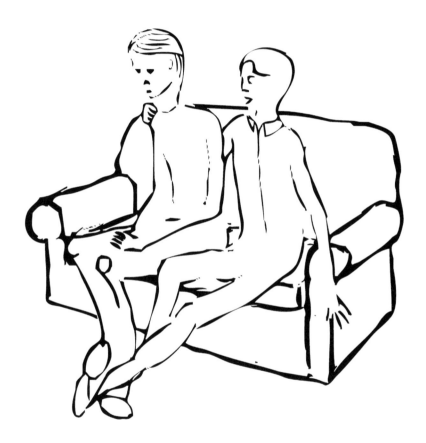

You seek help and support after a period of mourning.

Depression

You create an environment consistent with your feelings.

Action/Action Tendencies

Sadness

You maintain your environment regardless of your feelings.

...another drink

...and another

...and far too much to drink

..junk food

...and more junk

...really far too much junk food

A SELECTION OF SELF DESTRUCTION

BETBOB £100 to win on "Gift Horse"

...a gamble

BETBOB £100 to win on "Gift Horse"

...some more gambling

...far too much gambling

BETBOB £100 to win on "Gift Horse"

You attempt to terminate your feelings of depression in self destructive ways.

Sadness

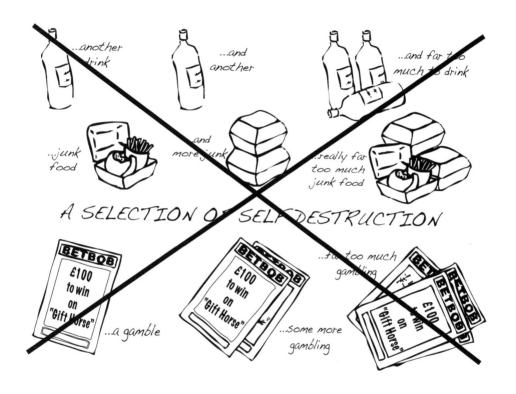

...another drink

...and another

...and far too much to drink

...junk food

...and more junk

...really far too much junk food

A SELECTION OF SELF DESTRUCTION

BETBOB £100 to win on "Gift Horse"

BETBOB £100 to win on "Gift Horse"

BETBOB £100 to win on "Gift Horse"

...far too much gambling

...a gamble

...some more gambling

You do not terminate your feelings in self destructive ways.

Now . . .

General Change or Philosophical Change for you?

General Change

STEP 1   Choose a typical example of your depression problem.

STEP 2   Identify your depression cognitive consequences and action tendencies and write them in your own words, using the illustrations as a guide. Make sure that they are specific to your example.

STEP 3   Identify your sadness cognitive consequences and action tendencies and write them in your own words, using the illustrations as a guide. Make sure they are specific to your example.

STEP 4   Commit to thinking and behaving in accordance with your healthy cognitive consequences and action tendencies for sadness.

STEP 5   Repeat, Repeat, Repeat in a consistent and forceful manner until your new thinking and your new behaviour become second nature.

Tip:
If behaving in accordance with healthy sadness is too overwhelming to begin with, then *imagine* yourself behaving in a healthy manner for a few weeks and then start in real life.

Philosophical Change

Remember to take your time if you are choosing this route, as Philosophical Change is about changing your unhealthy beliefs over the long term.

STEP 1   Identify your unhealthy belief.

STEP 2   Dispute your unhealthy belief.

STEP 3   Identify your healthy belief.

STEP 4   Dispute your healthy belief.

STEP 5   Strengthen your healthy belief and weaken your unhealthy belief

Remember, depression is provoked by unhealthy beliefs about loss or failure. An unhealthy belief is made up of absolutist **rigid beliefs** in the form of a MUST, HAVE TO, NEED TO, GOT TO, ABSOLUTELY SHOULD, from which three further derivative disturbed beliefs come.

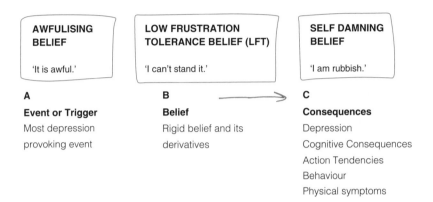

AWFULISING BELIEF

'It is awful.'

LOW FRUSTRATION TOLERANCE BELIEF (LFT)

'I can't stand it.'

SELF DAMNING BELIEF

'I am rubbish.'

A

Event or Trigger

Most depression provoking event

B

Belief

Rigid belief and its derivatives

C

Consequences

Depression

Cognitive Consequences

Action Tendencies

Behaviour

Physical symptoms

A rigid unhealthy belief, at **B**, is a demand about the most depressing aspect of an event – it is either a demand for it to **absolutely happen** or **absolutely not happen**.

For example, if what you are most depressed about is your depression, then the rigid belief is **I absolutely should not be feeling depression**. If what you are most depressed about is the end of a relationship, then the rigid belief is **I absolutely should still have my relationship**. The consequence of not having the rigid belief met is any or a combination of the three derivative beliefs.

For example:

RIGID BELIEF

'I must not be feeling depressed …'

AWFULISING BELIEF

'… it's awful that I am feeling depressed …'

LOW FRUSTRATION TOLERANCE BELIEF (LFT)

'… and I can't stand being depressed.'

SELF DAMNING BELIEF

'Being depressed proves I am rubbish.'

Step 1

Identify your unhealthy depression provoking belief

a. Choose a typical example of your depression problem.

b. Use the previous Common Depression Triggers table as a reference to pinpoint what you were *most* depressed about. You may have more than one trigger, which means you may have more than one depression provoking belief. Work on one belief at a time.

c. Express your answer to Question (b) above in the form of a 'MUST' or 'ABSOLUTELY SHOULD'. (See previous examples.)

d. Identify the three derivative beliefs. (Awfulising, Low Frustration Tolerance (LFT), Self Damning. See page 5 as a reminder to what these mean.)

You may have all three derivatives or any combination of the three.

Remember to imagine yourself in the trigger situation when identifying these derivative beliefs.

Examples	A	LFT	SD/OD
'I absolutely should not have been rejected; rejection is awful, unbearable and proves I'm worthless.'	✓	✓	✓
'I should not have failed; failure is awful, I can't stand it, it proves I am a failure.'	✓	✓	✓
'I must see an end to my depression; not seeing an end to it is awful and unbearable.'	✓	✓	
'I absolutely should not have lost my job; losing my job is awful, I can't stand it. I have no worth.'	✓	✓	✓

Key: A = Awfulising, LFT = Low Frustration Tolerance, SD = Self Damning, OD = Other Damning

Step 2

dispute? your unhealthy depression provoking belief

Question the validity of your unhealthy belief, using the following three criteria. Remember that an unhealthy belief is made up of the rigid belief and its derivatives. The disputing questions below are used on all of them.

a. Are they realistic or not and why?
b. Do they make sense or not and why?
c. Do they lead to helpful or unhelpful outcomes for me, and why?

Let's assume your unhealthy belief was as follows:

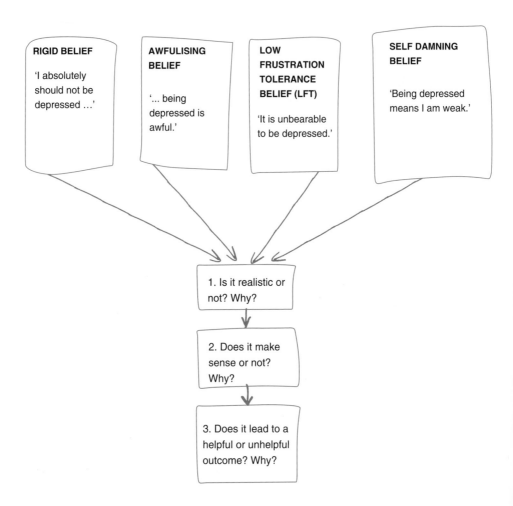

RIGID BELIEF

'I absolutely should not be depressed ...'

AWFULISING BELIEF

'... being depressed is awful.'

LOW FRUSTRATION TOLERANCE BELIEF (LFT)

'It is unbearable to be depressed.'

SELF DAMNING BELIEF

'Being depressed means I am weak.'

1. Is it realistic or not? Why?

2. Does it make sense or not? Why?

3. Does it lead to a helpful or unhelpful outcome? Why?

Go ahead and dispute your unhealthy belief or beliefs.

Step 3

Identify your healthy Sadness provoking belief

a. Change your unhealthy belief and work out the healthy version by removing the rigidity and replacing it with the preference belief.

b. Remember to negate your unhealthy demand. For example, 'I prefer not to be depressed but it doesn't mean that I must not be.'

c. Identify the derivative beliefs. (Anti-awfulising, High Frustration Tolerance (HFT), Self/Other/World Acceptance. See page 7 as a reminder to what these mean.) Use the examples below as a guide.

d. Remember, preference beliefs are flexible, make sense and lead to a helpful outcome.

Unhealthy beliefs	A	LFT	SD/OD
'I absolutely should not have been rejected; being rejected is awful, unbearable and proves I'm worthless.'	✓	✓	✓
'I should not have failed; failure is awful, I can't stand it, it proves I am a failure.'	✓	✓	✓
'I must see an end to my depression; not seeing an end to it is awful and unbearable.'	✓	✓	
'I absolutely should not have lost my job; losing my job is awful, I can't stand it. I have no worth.'	✓	✓	✓

Healthy versions	AA	HFT	SA/OA
'I would have preferred to have been accepted and not rejected but it doesn't mean that I absolutely must not be rejected. Being rejected is bad but not awful, difficult but not unbearable. It does not mean I'm worthless. I accept myself regardless.'	✓	✓	✓
'I would have liked not to have failed but it doesn't mean that I absolutely should not have. Failure is bad but not the end of the world, difficult but I can bear it. Failing does not make me a failure as a person. I'm fallible and I accept myself regardless.'	✓	✓	✓
'I would like to see an end to my depression but I doesn't mean that it must be so. Not seeing an end is bad but not awful, difficult but not unbearable.'	✓	✓	
'I would have liked not to have lost my job but I accept that I have. Losing my job is bad but not the end of the world, difficult but I am standing it. Losing my job does not make me a worthless person. My worth does not depend on the job. I accept myself regardless.'	✓	✓	✓

Key: A = Awfulising, LFT = Low Frustration Tolerance, SD = Self Damning,
OD = Other Damning, AA = Anti Awfulising, HFT = High Frustration Tolerance,
SA = Self Acceptance, OA = Other Acceptance

Go ahead and rewrite your beliefs in a healthy way.

Step 4

dispute? your healthy Sadness provoking belief

Dispute your healthy beliefs using the same criteria used in disputing the unhealthy beliefs – this keeps it fair and you are more likely to persuade yourself to commit to changing them if you dispute the unhealthy and the healthy beliefs in exactly the same way.

Remember that a healthy belief is made up of a preference belief and its three balanced derivatives or a combination of them. The disputing questions below are used on all of them.

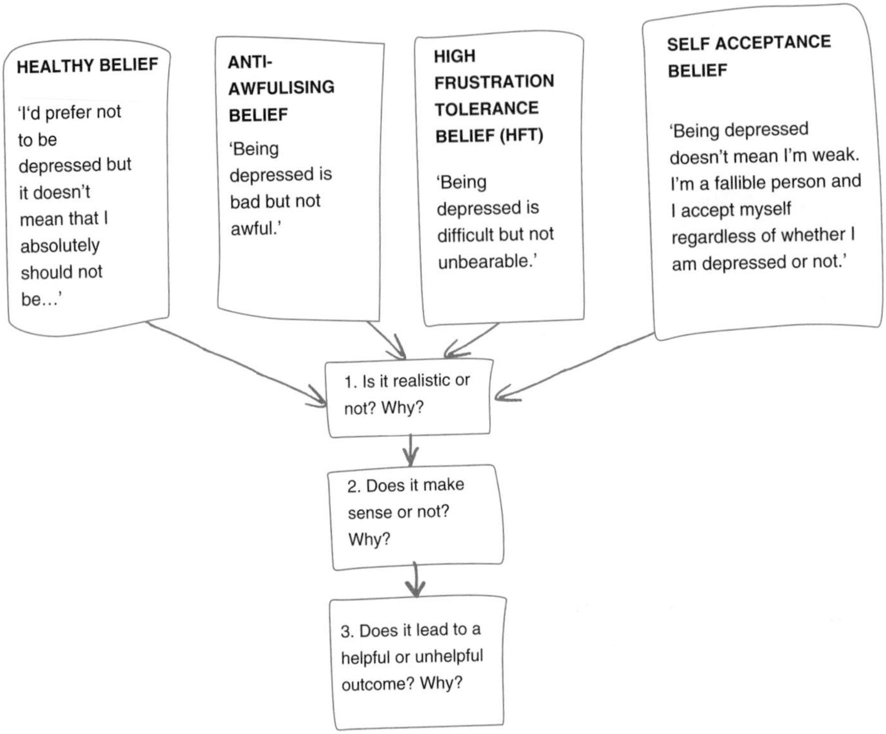

HEALTHY BELIEF

'I'd prefer not to be depressed but it doesn't mean that I absolutely should not be…'

ANTI-AWFULISING BELIEF

'Being depressed is bad but not awful.'

HIGH FRUSTRATION TOLERANCE BELIEF (HFT)

'Being depressed is difficult but not unbearable.'

SELF ACCEPTANCE BELIEF

'Being depressed doesn't mean I'm weak. I'm a fallible person and I accept myself regardless of whether I am depressed or not.'

1. Is it realistic or not? Why?

2. Does it make sense or not? Why?

3. Does it lead to a helpful or unhelpful outcome? Why?

Tip:
Remember that anti-awfulising is where 100% bad does not exist, as one can usually think of something worse.

Tip:
HFT means you have not disintegrated.

Tip:
Self/other acceptance is not dependent on conditions. We are all fallible human beings.

Go ahead and dispute your healthy belief and its balanced derivatives.

Step 5

STRENGTHEN your healthy Sadness provoking belief

weaken your unhealthy  provoking belief

In order to change your depression provoking belief to a healthy sadness provoking one, you need to think in accordance with your healthy belief and take constructive actions. The illustrations demonstrate the thinking (cognitive consequences) and action tendencies of sadness. The constructive actions are based on the action tendencies of sadness.

- Think and act in accordance with your healthy belief repeatedly and consistently in a forceful manner until eventually your emotional state changes from depression to sadness.

- Remember your emotion of depression **will** change – the new way of thinking and the new actions you will implement will feel uncomfortable initially but this is completely natural. You are changing an old habit of unhealthy thinking and old habitual depressive behaviours. It takes a few weeks of repetitions done consistently and forcefully.

- The behavioural goals you set for yourself need to be challenging but not overwhelming. If you overwhelm yourself then it defeats the object of the exercise.

- Start with imagining yourself thinking and acting in a healthy manner whilst being in the trigger situation until you think you are ready to challenge yourself in real life. For example, imagining yourself going out and meeting up with friends is a good start but at some point you will need to take action and make the arrangements and go and meet your friends and then continue until you achieve your desired goal.

- Recite your healthy belief in your head daily and particularly when you are imagining yourself in the trigger situation. This mental rehearsal will help you to remember it when you deliberately face the trigger situation in real life.

- Once you achieve your desired goal, whatever it is, then maintain the helpful thinking and actions. For example, if you are able to get to that big social event and then make no further arrangements to socialise you may begin to feel isolated again, so make efforts even when you don't feel like it.

- Review how you did, each time you challenge yourself, and then work out what you can do differently or better the next time. Then do it. Do not demand perfection from yourself. The process of moving from depression to sadness is uncomfortable and uneven. Some days you will make bigger strides when you challenge yourself and other days you will make small strides or even take a step back. The important thing is to accept that this can happen and then bring your focus back to what you are doing and continue with it.

- Remember, you didn't learn to drive a car, ride a bicycle or learn to read overnight, it takes repetition and focus and consistency.

Chapter 2 – Depression – Takeaway Tips

- To overcome depression, it is important to work with vigilance on self acceptance. Dispute your self damning beliefs energetically.

- Ensure you have good sleep hygiene and maintain regular routines. Go to bed at a reasonable hour in the evening and get up at a reasonable hour in the morning.

- Take regular exercise, ideally on a daily basis – this helps raise your energy levels.

- Eat regularly. It helps maintain a constant state of energy.

- Involve yourself in regular activities you enjoy. Read helpful, inspiring books, these help you keep a wider perspective on life rather than the narrow focus you tend to develop when you feel depressed.

- Challenge yourself but do not overwhelm yourself as you face your depression triggers.

CHAPTER 3

Anger and Annoyance

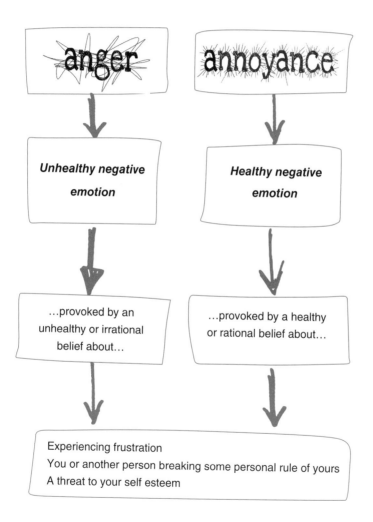

anger

annoyance

Unhealthy negative emotion

Healthy negative emotion

...provoked by an unhealthy or irrational belief about...

...provoked by a healthy or rational belief about...

Experiencing frustration
You or another person breaking some personal rule of yours
A threat to your self esteem

W e will focus on the most common triggers for anger and discuss some types of anger that are also experienced by many people.

Anger

You will have experienced some form of anger at some point in your life. It is a common emotion but it can be divided into two types of anger: unhealthy anger and healthy anger or annoyance. We will use the word 'anger' to mean unhealthy anger and 'annoyance' to mean healthy anger from now on. The intensity of both types can vary. Under anger you can experience hostility and rage. Annoyance can vary from mild irritation to intense annoyance.

Anger can be dangerous to the self or to another person. Anger leads to short and long term effects on your mental and physical health.

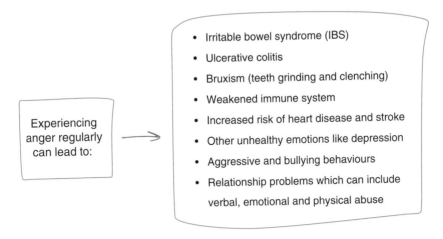

Experiencing anger regularly can lead to:

- Irritable bowel syndrome (IBS)
- Ulcerative colitis
- Bruxism (teeth grinding and clenching)
- Weakened immune system
- Increased risk of heart disease and stroke
- Other unhealthy emotions like depression
- Aggressive and bullying behaviours
- Relationship problems which can include verbal, emotional and physical abuse

In the Introduction, we talked about the three major MUSTs.

1. I *must* do well, greatly, perfectly, outstandingly and *must* win the approval of others or else it's awful, I can't stand it and I'm no good and I'll never do anything well. This can lead to anxiety, depression, despair and a sense of worthlessness, jealousy, hurt, unhealthy envy, guilt, shame and embarrassment and unhealthy anger with the self.
2. Other people *must* do the right thing or be a certain way or treat me well, or kindly or considerately and put me in the centre of their attention or else it's horrible, unbearable and proves they are bad and no good. This may lead to unhealthy anger, rage, hostility, resentment, jealousy and envy.
3. Life *must* be easy, without discomfort or inconvenience or any hassle or else it's horrible, unbearable, that damned world doesn't give me everything with ease and with no effort. This leads to low frustration tolerance, avoidance, procrastination, addiction, giving up on goals as well as anxiety and anger.

Most problems of anger stem from the second belief, that people MUST be a certain way. The first and second major MUSTs about the above triggers may result in anger with the self or anger with life and its hassles or anger with the world.

Expressing Anger

Anger can be expressed in different ways. It can be acted out immediately by shouting, throwing and breaking things and more dangerously by physical violence. Different people express their anger in different ways.

You may also suppress anger and then act in a passive aggressive manner by sulking, withdrawing, being obstructive, giving dirty looks, ignoring, manipulating, withholding information, making excuses and so on. A person behaving passive aggressively might not always show that they are angry. They might appear in agreement, polite, friendly but underneath they will be feeling angry.

At other times, anger is suppressed and then released in an aggressive burst. People who internalise and suppress their feelings may self harm when they are angry. This may give temporary relief from angry feelings, but it doesn't solve the problems in the long term and is destructive, which can lead to other emotional problems.

Unhelpful Strategies for Dealing with Anger

People deal with their anger in many different ways but unfortunately some of these strategies are not helpful in the long term. The following are examples of unhelpful solutions:

1. **Suppressing your anger** – Some people have a viewpoint that any type of anger is bad and should be suppressed, to keep the peace and avoid any conflict. A type of attitude based on 'I must always be nice and pleasant'. This is emotionally costly and leads to relationship problems, lack of personal fulfilment as well as physical symptoms. Some of our clients have even believed that having angry thoughts is a 'no no'. The problem is that we all feel angry and we all have angry thoughts and suppressing them only leads to more frustration and more angry thoughts. This becomes a vicious cycle: the harder you try to quash these feelings and thoughts the more persistent and intense they become; you then begin to put yourself down about them, leading to other emotional problems like guilt and depression.

2. **Just express your feelings or punch a cushion** – Some people have struggled with having and maintaining good relationships because they have firmly believed 'I'm an honest person and I have to be honest about how I feel all the time, you either take me or leave me'. The problem is that most of the time, others will not take them happily. If you have unhealthy beliefs about how others MUST treat you, then you will feel anger. The manner in which you will talk to another person will be hostile and 'finger pointing', leading to defensiveness by the other. This does not lead to a happy resolution of any conflict and is self defeating. You may also have read about taking your anger out on a cushion, or screaming at the top of your voice to release the pent up anger. This may provide temporary relief but it serves a similar purpose to self harm in that the problem is not solved, it is just delayed. You may think 'yes but it is not harmful to anyone' and you would be right but that doesn't alter the fact that the underlying unhealthy belief and destructive thoughts and attitudes remain unchanged so they will resurface next time you are triggered. Any type of immediate relief strategy will be ineffective in solving persistent anger and hostility problems if long term solutions are missing.

Anger Hurt

Anger hurt is a mixed emotion, felt when you think you have been treated unfairly or insensitively by someone you have an emotional connection with like a spouse, partner, friend, parent or sibling. The person feeling anger hurt usually notices and expresses the surface emotion of anger but by scraping this surface emotion we find that lurking deeper is hurt. The anger is triggered by an unhealthy belief about the other person and usually the other is judged as an uncaring, thoughtless, bad person for behaving in an unfair and insensitive manner but the hurt is triggered by an unhealthy belief about oneself. The hurt person rationalises and personalises the unfair or insensitive treatment as indicative that they are unlovable, worthless or not good enough.

Ego Defensive Anger

Ego defensive anger is when you perceive a threat to your self esteem. It is provoked when you receive criticism or when you think you have been criticised. The response is usually one of defensiveness and verbal attack. You may then withdraw and avoid the person you feel angry with. It is called ego defensive anger because if you acknowledge the criticism you would put yourself down for behaving in a manner that you absolutely MUST never do. The anger covers up the self damning belief. An example of a belief that provokes ego defensive anger is: 'You absolutely should not have criticised me. Your criticism reminds me that I am a failure or inadequate.'

Common Anger Triggers

The following are common triggers for anger and hostility. It is by no means an exhaustive list but it may help you understand your own specific triggers. Remember they may be about your demands of yourself or of others or of life.

Tick the box to identify your anger triggers

- ☐ Injustice
- ☐ Unfairness
- ☐ Disagreement
- ☐ Insensitivity
- ☐ Prejudices, e.g. religious, racial, gender, sexual orientation
- ☐ Being ignored
- ☐ Rudeness
- ☐ Disrespect
- ☐ Tone or manner of communication
- ☐ Making mistakes
- ☐ Not using talent
- ☐ Losing out
- ☐ Hurt feelings
- ☐ Not being competent, intelligent, wise
- ☐ Pain and suffering in the world
- ☐ Lack of control, whether it's managing to control your emotions, thoughts or behaviour
- ☐ Pain – physical and emotional
- ☐ Rejection
- ☐ Emotional problems like anxiety and depression
- ☐ Laziness
- ☐ Lying
- ☐ Not being listened to
- ☐ Being let down
- ☐ Someone not meeting your expectations
- ☐ Suffering a blow to your self esteem or your place within a social group
- ☐ Criticism
- ☐ Misinformation
- ☐ Abusive language/Insults
- ☐ Life hassles such as traffic congestion, weather etc.
- ☐ Humiliation, shaming, blaming
- ☐ Physical threat to self or loved ones
- ☐ Violation of your personal space
- ☐ Performance
- ☐ Failure and disappointment
- ☐ Lack of academic ability
- ☐ Not understanding something
- ☐ Other (write your own reason)

Am I Angry or Annoyed?

At the heart of your anger are unhealthy beliefs about

a. experiencing frustration
b. you or another person breaking some personal rule of yours, or
c. a threat to your self esteem.

Such irrational beliefs not only provoke anger but they have a consequence on how you think (cognitive consequences), act or tend to act (action tendencies). When you feel anger, for example, your thoughts may be how deliberately malicious the other person is being and you may feel like attacking them verbally or physically.

Assess if you are angry or annoyed by checking your cognitive consequences and action tendencies. Look through the illustrations and work out if you are angry or annoyed. It is important to put yourself in the trigger situation when you felt cross. It is easy to think that you don't have unhealthy beliefs and thoughts when you are no longer triggered. Imagine yourself in the trigger situation and then work out if you felt angry or annoyed.

You overestimate the extent to which the other person acted deliberately.

Cognitive Consequences

Annoyance

You do not overestimate the extent to which the other person acted deliberately.

Cognitive Consequences

Anger

You see malicious intent in the motives of others.

Cognitive Consequences

Annoyance

You don't see malicious intent in the motives of others.

Cognitive Consequences

Anger

You see yourself as definitely right; you see others as definitely wrong.

Cognitive Consequences

Annoyance

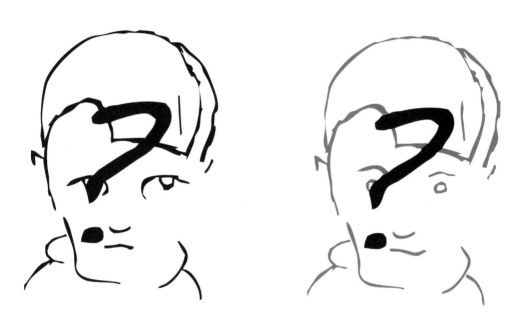

You do not see yourself as definitely right and others as definitely wrong.

Cognitive Consequences

Anger

You are unable to see the other person's point of view.

Cognitive Consequences

Annoyance

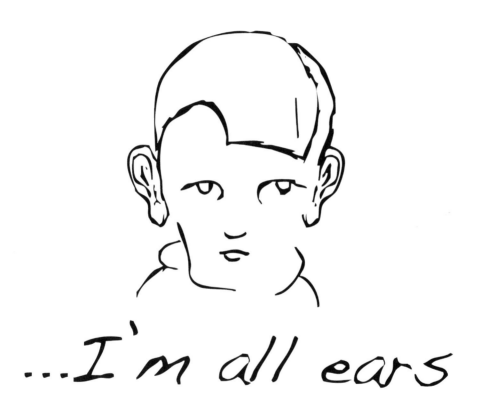

...I'm all ears

You are able to see the other person's point of view.

Cognitive Consequences

Anger

You plot to exact revenge.

Cognitive Consequences

Annoyance

You do not plot to exact revenge.

Anger

You attack the other person physically.

Annoyance

You assert yourself.

Action/Action Tendencies

Anger

You attack the other person verbally.

Annoyance

You request but do not demand behavioural change in the other person.

Anger

You attack the other person passive aggressively.

Annoyance

You do not attack the other person passive aggressively.

You displace your feelings by taking it out on something else.

Action/Action Tendencies

Annoyance

You do not displace feelings.

You withdraw aggressively.

Action/Action Tendencies

Annoyance

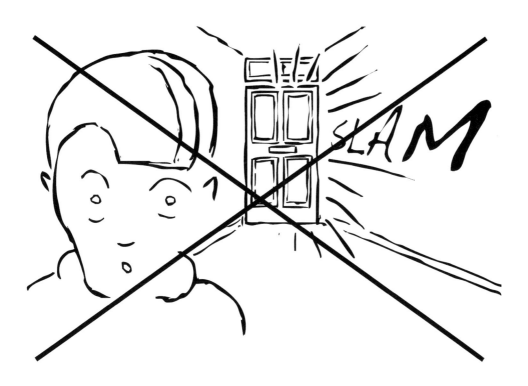

You do not withdraw aggressively.

Anger

You recruit allies against the other person.

Action/Action Tendencies

Annoyance

You do not recruit allies against the other person.

Now . . .

General Change or Philosophical Change for you?

General Change

STEP 1   Choose a typical example of your anger problem.

STEP 2   Identify your anger cognitive consequences and action tendencies and write them in your own words, using the illustrations as a guide. Make sure that they are specific to your example.

STEP 3   Identify your annoyance cognitive consequences and action tendencies and write them in your own words, using the illustrations as a guide. Make sure they are specific to your example.

STEP 4   Commit to thinking and behaving in accordance with your healthy cognitive consequences and action tendencies for annoyance.

STEP 5   Repeat, Repeat, Repeat in a consistent and forceful manner until your new thinking and your new behaviour become second nature.

> **Tip:**
> If behaving in accordance with healthy annoyance is too overwhelming to begin with, then *imagine* yourself behaving in a healthy manner for a few weeks and then start in real life.

Philosophical Change

Remember to take your time if you are choosing this route, as Philosophical Change is about changing your unhealthy beliefs over the long term.

STEP 1   Identify your unhealthy belief.

STEP 2   Dispute your unhealthy belief.

STEP 3   Work out your healthy version of your belief.

STEP 4   Dispute your healthy belief.

STEP 5   Strengthen your healthy belief and weaken your unhealthy belief.

Remember, anger is provoked by unhealthy beliefs about (i) experiencing frustration, (ii) you or another person breaking some personal rule of yours and (iii) a threat to your self esteem. An unhealthy belief is made up of absolutist **rigid beliefs** in the form of a MUST, HAVE TO, NEED TO, GOT TO, ABSOLUTELY SHOULD, from which three further derivative disturbed beliefs come.

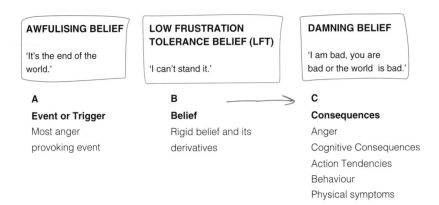

A rigid unhealthy belief, at **B**, is a demand about the most anger provoking aspect of an event – it is either a demand for it to **absolutely happen** or **absolutely not happen**.

For example, if what you are most angry about is being ignored, then the rigid belief is **you absolutely should not have ignored me**. If what you are most angry about is being treated unfairly, then the rigid belief is **you absolutely must treat me fairly**. The consequences of not having the rigid belief met are any or a combination of the three derivative beliefs.

For example:

RIGID BELIEF	AWFULISING BELIEF	LOW FRUSTRATION TOLERANCE BELIEF (LFT)	OTHER DAMNING BELIEF
'You must treat me fairly.'	'Being treated unfairly by you is awful'	'and being treated unfairly by you is unbearable'	'and being treated unfairly by you proves you are a bad or worthless person'

Step 1

Identify your unhealthy ~~anger~~ provoking belief

a. Choose a typical example of your anger problem.

b. Use the previous Common Anger Triggers table as a reference to pinpoint what you were most angry about. You may have more than one trigger, which means you may have more than one anger provoking belief. Work on one belief at a time.

c. Express your answer to Question (b) above in the form of a 'MUST'. (See previous examples.)

d. Identify the three derivative beliefs. (Awfulising, Low Frustration Tolerance (LFT), Self Damning. See page 5 as a reminder to what these mean.)

You may have all three derivatives or any combination of the three.

Remember to imagine yourself in the trigger situation when identifying these derivative beliefs.

Examples	A	LFT	SD/OD
'You must treat me fairly; being treated unfairly by you is awful, unbearable and makes you a bad person.'	✓	✓	✓
'You absolutely should have spoken to me politely; I can't stand the fact that you didn't.'		✓	
'You must treat me in exactly the same way I treat you; the fact you don't is awful and unbearable.'	✓	✓	
'I must always do the right thing; it's awful that I didn't recently, I can't stand it when I don't, I'm stupid and useless.'	✓	✓	✓

Key: A = Awfulising, LFT = Low Frustration Tolerance, SD = Self Damning, OD = Other Damning

Step 2

dispute? your unhealthy ~~anger~~ provoking belief

Question the validity of your unhealthy belief, using the following three criteria. Remember that an unhealthy belief is made up of the rigid belief and its derivatives. The disputing questions below are used on all of them.

a. Are they realistic or not and why?
b. Do they make sense or not and why?
c. Do they lead to helpful or unhelpful outcomes for me, and why?

Let's assume your unhealthy belief was as follows:

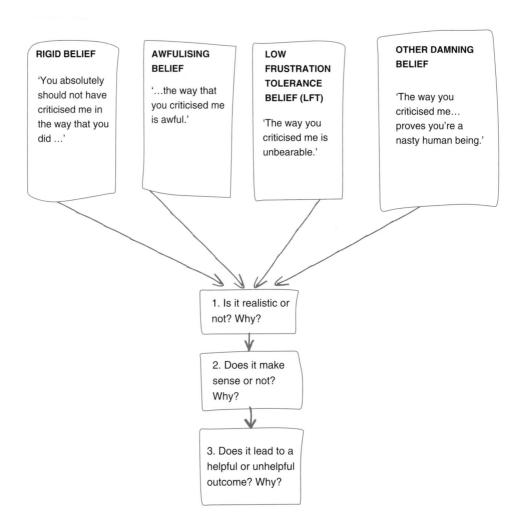

RIGID BELIEF

'You absolutely should not have criticised me in the way that you did …'

AWFULISING BELIEF

'…the way that you criticised me is awful.'

LOW FRUSTRATION TOLERANCE BELIEF (LFT)

'The way you criticised me is unbearable.'

OTHER DAMNING BELIEF

'The way you criticised me… proves you're a nasty human being.'

1. Is it realistic or not? Why?

2. Does it make sense or not? Why?

3. Does it lead to a helpful or unhelpful outcome? Why?

Go ahead and dispute your unhealthy belief or beliefs.

Step 3

Identify your healthy annoyance provoking belief

a. Change your unhealthy belief and work out the healthy version by removing the rigidity and replacing it with the preference belief.
b. Remember to negate your unhealthy demand. For example, 'I want to be treated fairly but I absolutely don't have to be'.
c. Identify the derivative beliefs. (Anti-awfulising, High Frustration Tolerance (HFT), Self/Other/World Acceptance. See page 7 as a reminder to what these mean.) Use the examples below as a guide.
d. Remember, preference beliefs are flexible, make sense and lead to a helpful outcome.

Unhealthy beliefs	A	LFT	SD/OD
'You must treat me fairly. Being treated unfairly by you is awful and unbearable and makes you a bad person.'	✓	✓	✓
'You absolutely should have spoken to me politely. I can't stand the fact that you didn't.'		✓	
'You must treat me in exactly the same way I treat you; the fact you don't is awful and unbearable.'	✓	✓	
'I must always do the right thing. It's awful that I didn't recently, I can't stand it when I don't, I'm stupid and useless.'	✓	✓	✓

Healthy versions	AA	HFT	SA/OA
'I would have liked to have been treated fairly by you, but it doesn't mean that I absolutely should have been. Being treated unfairly is bad but not awful, frustrating but not unbearable, it doesn't prove you're a bad person, despite your bad behaviour. You are fallible like all of us.'	✓	✓	✓
'I would have preferred you speaking to me politely but it doesn't mean that you absolutely should have. I am frustrated but I can handle it.'		✓	
'I'd rather you treated me in the same way I treat you but there's no law of nature that says that you absolutely should. It's bad that you don't but not awful, difficult but I can deal with it.'	✓	✓	
'I'd like to always do the right thing but I accept that I don't always do it. It's frustrating when I don't but not intolerable, it doesn't mean I'm stupid or useless. I'm fallible. I accept myself unconditionally.'	✓	✓	✓

Key: A = Awfulising, LFT = Low Frustration Tolerance, SD = Self Damning, OD = Other Damning, AA = Anti Awfulising, HFT = High Frustration Tolerance, SA = Self Acceptance, OA = Other Acceptance

Go ahead and rewrite your beliefs in a healthy way.

Step 4

dispute? your healthy annoyance provoking belief

Dispute your healthy beliefs using the same criteria used in disputing the unhealthy beliefs – this keeps it fair and you are more likely to persuade yourself to commit to changing them if you dispute the unhealthy and the healthy beliefs in exactly the same way.

Remember that a healthy belief is made up of a preference belief and its three balanced derivatives or a combination of them. The disputing questions below are used on all of them.

HEALTHY BELIEF

'I'd have liked it if you hadn't criticised me in the way that you did but it doesn't mean that you absolutely should not have.'

ANTI-AWFULISING BELIEF

'The fact that you criticised me in that way is bad but not awful.'

HIGH FRUSTRATION TOLERANCE BELIEF (HFT)

'The way you criticised me was difficult for me but not unbearable.'

OTHER ACCEPTANCE BELIEF

'The fact that you criticised me in that way doesn't prove you're a nasty human being. You are fallible like the rest of us.'

1. Is it realistic or not? Why?

2. Does it make sense or not? Why?

3. Does it lead to a helpful or unhelpful outcome? Why?

Tip:
Remember that anti-awfulising is where 100% bad does not exist, as one can usually think of something worse.

Tip:
HFT means you have not disintegrated.

Tip:
Self/other acceptance is not dependent on conditions. We are all fallible human beings.

Go ahead and dispute your healthy belief and its balanced derivatives.

Step 5

STRENGTHEN your healthy annoyance provoking belief

weaken your unhealthy anger provoking belief

In order to change your anger provoking belief to a healthy annoyance provoking one, you need to think in accordance with your healthy belief and take constructive actions. The illustrations demonstrate the thinking (cognitive consequences) and action tendencies of annoyance. The constructive actions are based on the action tendencies of annoyance.

- Think and act in accordance with your healthy belief repeatedly and consistently in a forceful manner until eventually your emotional state changes from anger to a healthy annoyance.

- Remember your emotion of anger **will** change – the new way of thinking and the new actions you will implement will feel uncomfortable initially but this is completely natural. You are changing an old habit of unhealthy thinking and old habitual angry behaviours. It takes a few weeks of repetitions done consistently and forcefully.

- The behavioural goals you set for yourself need to be challenging but not overwhelming. If you overwhelm yourself then it defeats the object of the exercise.

- Start with imagining yourself thinking and acting in a healthy manner whilst being in the trigger situation until you think you are ready to challenge yourself in real life. For example, imagining yourself in the anger provoking situation being assertive rather than aggressive is a good start. At some point you will need to take action and behave assertively in that same situation. You will then need to continue behaving assertively until you achieve your desired goal of communicating effectively.

- Repeat your healthy belief in your head daily and particularly when you are imagining yourself in the trigger situation. This mental rehearsal will help you to remember it when you deliberately face the trigger situation in real life.

- Once you achieve your desired goal, whatever it is, then you need to maintain the helpful thinking and actions. For example, if you achieve your goal of being assertive in the given situation, continue to act in this way.

- Review how you did, each time you challenge yourself, and then work out what you can do differently or better the next time. Then do it. Do not demand perfection from yourself. The process of moving from anger to annoyance is uncomfortable and uneven. Some days you will make bigger strides when you challenge yourself and other days you will make small strides or even take a step back. The important thing is to accept that this can happen and then bring your focus back to what you are doing and continue with it.

- Remember, you didn't learn to drive a car, ride a bicycle or learn to read overnight, it takes repetition and focus and consistency.

Chapter 3 – Anger – Takeaway Tips

- Stop and think. When you start to feel the first tell-tale signs of anger stirrings, stop and think for a moment. Recite your healthy belief in your head. This will give you time to remember to think in a healthy manner.

- Remove yourself from the situation if you are overwhelmed with anger. If you feel you're feeling extreme anger and feeling that you want to lash out at someone, remove yourself from the situation. Sit down and work out your unhealthy belief and dispute it.

- Resolve conflict or unresolved issues. This is helpful for you in the long term too. First go through the change process in this chapter.

- Express your feelings in the right way. When you feel frustrated or irritated, take ownership of your feelings and tell people 'I'm feeling annoyed, frustrated about . . .'. Avoid expressions like 'You make me so angry', or 'You are so rude'. Talk slowly and clearly and ask rather than make demands. You are more likely to be listened to this way.

- Good communication skills can help you get your message across. Keep the lines of communication open. Listen to other people's point of view even if you don't agree. Making assumptions without evidence can create a problem where there is none.

CHAPTER 4

Guilt and Remorse

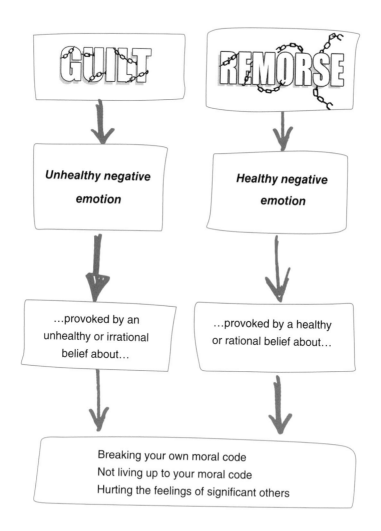

Unhealthy negative emotion

Healthy negative emotion

...provoked by an unhealthy or irrational belief about...

...provoked by a healthy or rational belief about...

Breaking your own moral code
Not living up to your moral code
Hurting the feelings of significant others

We will focus on some common issues that we've observed in our private practice regarding guilt.

Guilt

Guilt is an unhealthy negative emotion. We have all experienced it. If you hold unhealthy beliefs about moral rules and you act against them, then you will feel guilt. Generally speaking, guilt is experienced silently and often no one knows you are experiencing it. It is about you thinking that you have committed a sin, so to speak, but with the following mindset:

a. I have done something morally wrong.
b. I absolutely should not have done the wrong deed.
c. I am a bad person because of it.

When you feel guilt, you accept responsibility for your 'morally' wrong deed. This is not a bad thing to do but then you go on to judge yourself in a harsh way without considering the circumstances under which the 'sin' was committed. Taking responsibility in this way becomes self blame.

Remorse, on the other hand, is triggered by the following mindset:

a. I have done something morally wrong.
b. I wish I hadn't done the wrong thing.
c. I accept that I have done something I deem as morally wrong.
d. I'm a fallible person.
e. I did the wrong thing under these circumstances.
f. I will make amends and ask for forgiveness if that is possible or appropriate.

With remorse, responsibility is accepted but without self damning. When you feel remorse you accept your imperfection and look for ways to make amends. This does not mean letting yourself off the hook. It simply means that in most situations, but not all, there are some external stressors that need to be taken into consideration to be balanced and fair.

For example, you may feel guilt if you did not visit a friend in hospital more than once but you do not take into consideration that you were working extremely long hours because of important deadlines. Remorse takes such external factors into consideration.

There are times when you may not be able to make amends or even ask the person you have wronged for forgiveness. This may be due to death or the other person cutting all contact with you. If you are experiencing this or something similar then you will need to forgive yourself. No one is perfect and we all make mistakes. It is important to learn from such an experience and accept your fallibility in order to heal yourself from the guilt feeling.

Guilt can be experienced about specific actions or lack of actions; it can also be experienced and is sometimes known as 'existential guilt' when you become aware of a discrepancy between your well-being and the well-being of others. For example, 'I am bad because I'm better off than my brother, and I absolutely shouldn't be'.

We generally gain our moral compass from family, religion, the cultures and the societies we live in. If we transgress our moral codes and we hold rigid views about them, then we will feel guilt.

Common Guilt Triggers

The following are common triggers of guilt – the list is not exhaustive. Tick the boxes that you think apply to you.

Tick the box to identify your guilt triggers

- ☐ Doing something wrong
- ☐ Letting someone significant down
- ☐ Keeping secrets
- ☐ Secretive behaviour
- ☐ Thinking about what you have done wrong
- ☐ Feeling angry towards someone
- ☐ Being reminded of a past bad behaviour
- ☐ Hurting someone you care about
- ☐ Breaking your moral code
- ☐ Committing a sin
- ☐ Telling lies
- ☐ Being late consistently and feeling guilty about it
- ☐ Laughing at someone else's misfortune
- ☐ Losing connection with significant others
- ☐ Failure
- ☐ Not behaving responsibly
- ☐ Infidelity
- ☐ Feeling pleasure including sexual pleasure
- ☐ Being happy or having a feeling of well-being
- ☐ Having a helper, e.g. cleaner, gardener etc.
- ☐ Spending money or purchasing something
- ☐ Flirting
- ☐ Thinking about a sin or fantasising
- ☐ Other (write your own reason)

Am I Feeling Guilt or Remorse?

Guilt is provoked by unhealthy beliefs about the fact you have gone against your moral code or hurt a significant other in your life.

Such unhealthy beliefs not only provoke guilt but they have a consequence on how you think (cognitive consequences) and also impact on what you feel like doing (action tendencies). When you feel guilt, for example, your thoughts may be preoccupied with 'I'm a bad person' and you will feel like punishing yourself.

Assess if you are feeling guilt or remorse by checking your cognitive consequences and action tendencies.

Look through the illustrations for the cognitive consequences and action tendencies and work out if you are feeling guilt or remorse. It is important to put yourself in the trigger situation when you feel guilt. It is easy to think that you don't have unhealthy beliefs and thoughts when you are not triggered or when you are not thinking about your transgression. Imagine yourself in the situation or in the mindset that triggered your feelings, then work out if your feelings are healthy or unhealthy, i.e. guilt or remorse.

Cognitive Consequences

Guilt

You assume that you have definitely committed the sin.

Cognitive Consequences

Remorse

You consider your behaviour in context and with understanding in making final judgement concerning whether you have actually sinned.

Cognitive Consequences

Guilt

You assume more personal responsibility than the situation warrants.

Cognitive Consequences

Remorse

You assume an appropriate level of personal responsibility.

Cognitive Consequences

Guilt

You assign far less responsibility to others than is warranted.

Cognitive Consequences

Remorse

You assign the appropriate level of responsibility to others.

Cognitive Consequences

Guilt

You do not think of mitigating factors.

Cognitive Consequences

Remorse

You take into account mitigating factors.

Guilt

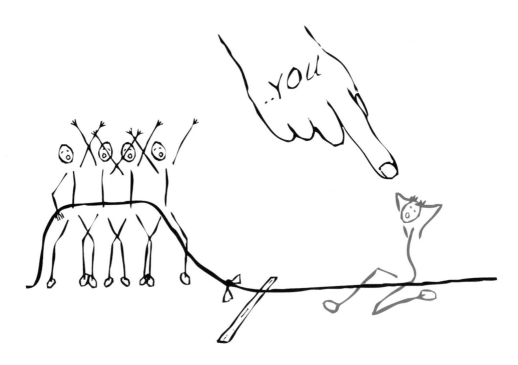

You think that you will receive retribution.

Cognitive Consequences

Remorse

You do not think you will receive retribution.

Guilt

You try to escape from the unhealthy pain of guilt in self defeating ways.

Remorse

You face up to the healthy pain that accompanies the realisation that you have sinned.

You beg for forgiveness from the person involved.

Remorse

You ask but do not beg for forgiveness.

You promise unrealistically that you will never sin again.

Remorse

You understand reasons for wrongdoing and act on your understanding.

You punish yourself physically or by deprivation.

Remorse

You atone for the sin by taking a penalty.

Guilt

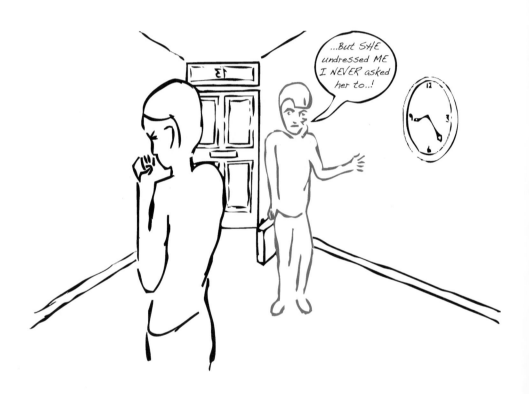

You disclaim responsibility for your wrongdoing.

Action/Action Tendencies

Remorse

You make appropriate amends.

Guilt

You have a tendency to make excuses for your behaviour or enact other defensive behaviour.

Action/Action Tendencies

Remorse

You have no tendency to make excuses for your behaviour or enact other defensive behaviours.

Now . . .

General Change or Philosophical Change for you?

General Change

STEP 1   Choose a typical example of your guilt problem.

STEP 2   Identify your guilt cognitive consequences and action tendencies and write them in your own words, using the illustrations as a guide. Make sure that they are specific to your example.

STEP 3   Identify your remorse cognitive consequences and action tendencies and write them in your own words, using the illustrations as a guide. Make sure they are specific to your example.

STEP 4   Commit to thinking and behaving in accordance with your healthy cognitive consequences and action tendencies for remorse.

STEP 5   Repeat, Repeat, Repeat in a consistent and forceful manner until your new thinking and your new behaviour become second nature.

Tip:
If behaving in accordance with healthy remorse is too overwhelming to begin with, then *imagine* yourself behaving in a healthy manner for a few weeks and then start in real life.

Philosophical Change

Remember to take your time if you are choosing this route, as Philosophical Change is about changing your unhealthy beliefs over the long term.

STEP 1   Identify your unhealthy belief.

STEP 2   Dispute your unhealthy belief.

STEP 3   Work out the healthy version of your belief.

STEP 4   Dispute your healthy belief.

STEP 5   Strengthen your healthy belief and weaken your unhealthy belief.

Remember, guilt is provoked by unhealthy beliefs about violation of, or failure to live up to, your moral codes and about hurting the feelings of a significant other. An unhealthy belief is made up of absolutist **rigid beliefs** in the form of a MUST, HAVE TO, NEED TO, GOT TO, ABSOLUTELY SHOULD, from which three further derivative disturbed beliefs come.

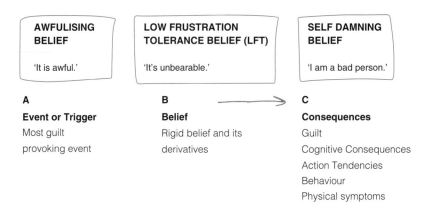

AWFULISING BELIEF	LOW FRUSTRATION TOLERANCE BELIEF (LFT)	SELF DAMNING BELIEF
'It is awful.'	'It's unbearable.'	'I am a bad person.'

A	**B**	**C**
Event or Trigger	**Belief**	**Consequences**
Most guilt provoking event	Rigid belief and its derivatives	Guilt
		Cognitive Consequences
		Action Tendencies
		Behaviour
		Physical symptoms

A rigid unhealthy belief, at **B**, is a demand about the most guilt provoking aspect of an event – it is either a demand for it to **absolutely happen** or **absolutely not happen**.

For example, if what you are most guilty about is infidelity, then the rigid belief is **I absolutely should have been faithful** or **I absolutely should not have been unfaithful**. If what you are most guilty about is not acting responsibly, then the rigid belief is **I absolutely should have acted responsibly**. The consequences of not having the rigid belief met are any or a combination of the three derivative beliefs.

For example:

RIGID BELIEF	AWFULISING BELIEF	LOW FRUSTRATION TOLERANCE BELIEF (LFT)	SELF DAMNING BELIEF
'I absolutely SHOULD have been faithful.'	'The fact that I wasn't faithful is awful.'	'The fact that I wasn't faithful is unbearable.'	'The fact that I wasn't faithful proves I am a bad person.'

Step 1

Identify your unhealthy GUILT provoking belief

a. Choose a typical example of your guilt problem.

b. Use the previous Common Guilt Triggers table as a reference to pinpoint what you were most guilty about. You may have more than one trigger, which means you may have more than one guilt provoking belief. Work on one belief at a time.

c. Express your answer to Question (b) above in the form of a 'MUST'. (See previous examples.)

d. Identify the three derivative beliefs. (Awfulising, Low Frustration Tolerance, Self Damning. See page 5 as a reminder to what these mean.)

You may have all three derivatives or any combination of the three.

Remember to imagine yourself in the trigger situation when identifying these derivative beliefs.

Examples	A	LFT	SD/OD
'I should not have let people down. It's awful that I did, I can't stand it, I'm a bad person.'	✓	✓	✓
'I absolutely should have been faithful to my partner. The fact that I wasn't proves I'm a terrible human being and bad.'			✓
'I should always act in a responsible way; acting irresponsibly is terrible and unbearable. I am a bad person.'	✓	✓	✓
'I should always do what I say I will. When I don't it's unbearable and means I am not a good enough person.'		✓	✓

Key: A = Awfulising, LFT = Low Frustration Tolerance, SD = Self Damning,
OD = Other Damning

Step 2

dispute? your unhealthy GUILT provoking belief

Question the validity of your unhealthy belief, using the following three criteria. Remember that an unhealthy belief is made up of the rigid belief and its derivatives. The disputing questions below are used on all of them.

a. Are they realistic or not and why?
b. Do they make sense or not and why?
c. Do they lead to helpful or unhelpful outcomes for me, and why?

Let's assume your unhealthy belief was as follows:

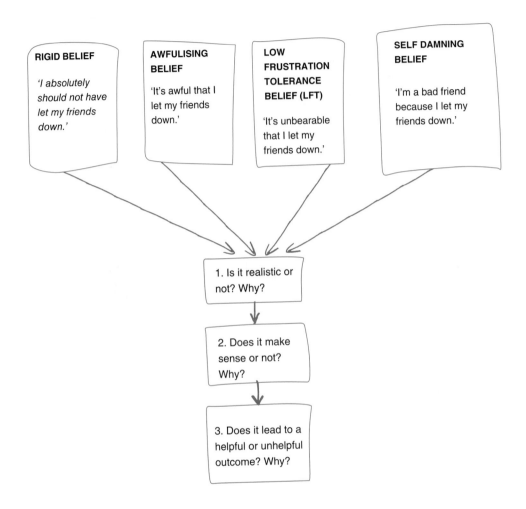

RIGID BELIEF

'I absolutely should not have let my friends down.'

AWFULISING BELIEF

'It's awful that I let my friends down.'

LOW FRUSTRATION TOLERANCE BELIEF (LFT)

'It's unbearable that I let my friends down.'

SELF DAMNING BELIEF

'I'm a bad friend because I let my friends down.'

1. Is it realistic or not? Why?

2. Does it make sense or not? Why?

3. Does it lead to a helpful or unhelpful outcome? Why?

Go ahead and dispute your unhealthy belief or beliefs.

Step 3

Identify your healthy REMORSE provoking belief

a. Change your unhealthy belief and work out the healthy version by removing the rigidity and replacing it with the preference belief.

b. Remember to negate your unhealthy demand. For example, 'I prefer to always do what I say I am going to do but I don't have to'.

c. Identify the derivative beliefs. (Anti-awfulising, High Frustration Tolerance (HFT), Self/Other/World Acceptance. See page 7 as a reminder to what these mean.) Use the examples below as a guide.

d. Remember, preference beliefs are flexible, make sense and lead to a helpful outcome.

Unhealthy beliefs	A	LFT	SD/OD
'I absolutely should not have let people down. It's awful that I did, I can't stand it, I'm a bad person.'	✓	✓	✓
'I absolutely should have been faithful to my partner. The fact that I wasn't proves I'm a terrible human being and bad.'			✓
'I should always act in a responsible way; acting irresponsibly is terrible and unbearable. I am a bad person.'	✓	✓	✓
'I should always do what I say I will. When I don't it's unbearable and means I am not a good enough person.'		✓	✓

Healthy versions	AA	HFT	SA/OA
'I would have preferred not to have let people down, but it doesn't mean that I absolutely must not, that I did is bad but not awful, it's difficult but I'm bearing it. It doesn't mean I am a bad person, I accept myself as a fallible human being. I will make amends and learn from this.'	✓	✓	✓
'I wish I had not been unfaithful to my partner but it doesn't mean that I absolutely must not. I behaved very badly but I'm not a bad person. I'm not perfect. I will make amends, do the right thing and learn from this.'			✓
'I'd like to act responsibly all the time but it doesn't mean that I absolutely must; the fact that I acted irresponsibly is bad but not awful, difficult but tolerable. It doesn't make me a bad person. It makes me a fallible person. I will make amends and learn from this.'	✓	✓	✓
'I prefer to do as I say I will, but I don't have to. The fact that I didn't do what I said I would is really difficult for me but I can bear it. It doesn't mean I'm not good enough. I'm not perfect. I will make amends, apologise and do the right thing.'		✓	✓

Key: A = Awfulising, LFT = Low Frustration Tolerance, SD = Self Damning,
OD = Other Damning, AA = Anti Awfulising, HFT = High Frustration Tolerance,
SA = Self Acceptance, OA = Other Acceptance

Go ahead and rewrite your beliefs in a healthy way.

Step 4

Dispute your healthy beliefs using the same criteria used in disputing the unhealthy beliefs – this keeps it fair and you are more likely to persuade yourself to commit to changing them if you dispute the unhealthy and the healthy beliefs in exactly the same way.

Remember that a healthy belief is made up of a preference belief and its three balanced derivatives or a combination of them. The disputing questions below are used on all of them.

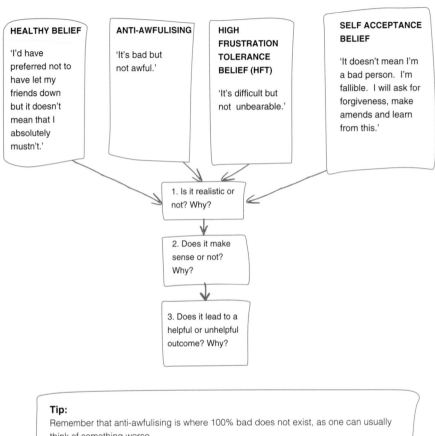

HEALTHY BELIEF

'I'd have preferred not to have let my friends down but it doesn't mean that I absolutely mustn't.'

ANTI-AWFULISING

'It's bad but not awful.'

HIGH FRUSTRATION TOLERANCE BELIEF (HFT)

'It's difficult but not unbearable.'

SELF ACCEPTANCE BELIEF

'It doesn't mean I'm a bad person. I'm fallible. I will ask for forgiveness, make amends and learn from this.'

1. Is it realistic or not? Why?

2. Does it make sense or not? Why?

3. Does it lead to a helpful or unhelpful outcome? Why?

Tip:
Remember that anti-awfulising is where 100% bad does not exist, as one can usually think of something worse.

Tip:
HFT means you have not disintegrated.

Tip:
Self/other acceptance is not dependent on conditions. We are all fallible human beings.

Go ahead and dispute your healthy belief and its balanced derivatives.

Step 5

weaken your unhealthy GUILT provoking belief

In order to change your guilt provoking belief to a healthy remorse provoking one, you need to think in accordance with your healthy belief and take constructive actions. The illustrations demonstrate the thinking (cognitive consequences) and action tendencies of remorse. The constructive actions are based on the action tendencies of remorse.

- Think and act in accordance with your healthy belief repeatedly and consistently in a forceful manner until eventually your emotional state changes from guilt to remorse.

- Remember your emotion of guilt **will** change – the new way of thinking and the new actions you will implement will feel uncomfortable initially but this is completely natural. You are changing an old habit of unhealthy thinking and old habitual guilty behaviours. It takes a few weeks of repetitions done consistently and forcefully.

- The behavioural goals you set for yourself need to be challenging but not overwhelming. If you overwhelm yourself then it defeats the object of the exercise.

- Start with imagining yourself thinking and acting in a healthy manner whilst being in the trigger situation until you think you are ready to challenge yourself in real life. For example, imagining yourself asking for forgiveness or making amends is a good start but at some point you will need to take action and do it.

- Repeat your healthy belief in your head daily and particularly when you are imagining yourself in the trigger situation. This mental rehearsal will help you to remember it when you deliberately face the trigger situation in real life.

- Once you achieve your desired goal, whatever it is, then you need to maintain the helpful thinking and actions. This means keeping the philosophies of remorse alive.

- Review how you did, each time you challenge yourself, and then work out what you can do differently or better the next time. Then do it. Do not demand perfection from yourself. The process of moving from guilt to remorse is uncomfortable and uneven. Some days you will make bigger strides when you challenge yourself and other days you will make small strides or even take a step back. The important thing is to accept that this can happen and then bring your focus back to what you are doing and continue with it.

- Remember, you didn't learn to drive a car, ride a bicycle or learn to read overnight, it takes repetition and focus and consistency.

Chapter 4 – Guilt – Takeaway Tips

- Become and remain aware of your values and the moral code you wish to apply to your life but don't hold your values rigidly. No one is perfect.

- Take responsibility for your actions and acknowledge any transgression and then ask for forgiveness, make amends and learn from it.

- If asking for forgiveness or making amends is no longer an option, then forgive yourself and accept that you are a fallible human being who has made a mistake. Learn from it.

- Make self reflection a habit.

- Keep a healthy work–life balance to ensure time for reflection.

CHAPTER 5

Hurt and Disappointment

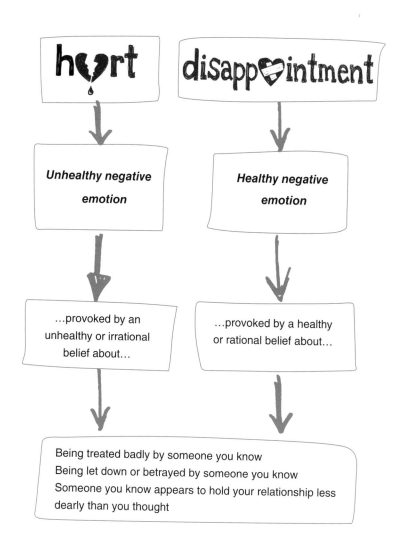

We will focus on some common triggers for hurt that we've observed in our private practice.

Hurt

Hurt is felt strongly in significant relationships, i.e. family, intimate relationships, friendships, work situations. It is not usually experienced with strangers, though it can happen. Hurt is about the theme of care, love and consideration. What you feel hurt about can vary within the various relationships you have because you will hold different expectations about how you want to be treated within each. You may feel hurt if a close friend asked another mutual friend to go on holiday with them instead of you but you may not feel hurt if your manager asked another colleague of yours to lead a project instead of you, you might feel relief.

Some people feel predominantly hurt whilst others feel a number of different emotions alongside their feeling of hurt. In Chapter 3, for example, we mentioned 'anger hurt', where anger is, usually, experienced when you put down the person who has treated you badly and hurt is, usually, felt when you put yourself down. You can also experience anger hurt without damning the other or yourself but when you feel like your bad treatment is unbearable. In our clinical practice we find anger hurt is felt predominantly when you put the other person down for treating you badly but you also put yourself down, as you think the reason you were treated badly was because you are unworthy or unlovable.

Example: Anger Hurt

1. You absolutely should not have treated me badly. You are a bad, thoughtless person.
2. You absolutely should not have treated me badly. The fact that you did proves I'm unlovable.

The first unhealthy belief triggers anger; the second triggers hurt.

Associated with hurt are thoughts about not deserving the bad treatment. Whether we deserve something or not is purely subjective. The idea behind 'deserving' is based on reciprocity; if I treat someone well and with consideration then I 'deserve' to be treated the same way. Unfortunately, there is no such Law of the Universe. Life and people do not operate in this manner. It would be great if we were always considerate, thoughtful and treated one another with care but sadly this is not reality. It is more helpful for us to think that even if we treat someone well, it does not follow that the same MUST happen back to us, even though we'd strongly prefer it.

Meta-emotions of Hurt

A meta-emotion is an emotional problem about an emotional problem. For example, you can feel anxious about feeling hurt, depressed about feeling hurt, angry with yourself about getting hurt and shame or embarrassment about feeling hurt. You will know if you have a meta-emotion about your hurt feelings by asking yourself 'how do I feel about my hurt feelings?'

Anxiety about Hurt

Anxiety about hurt is provoked by the unhealthy belief 'I must not feel hurt' because feeling hurt is awful, unbearable or proves that I am worthless (or some other form of self damning belief). It is possible to have these three derivative beliefs or any combination of them. If you feel anxious about feeling hurt then you will need to work through these feelings of anxiety as well as feelings of hurt. You can refer back to Chapter 1 if you want to work on your feelings of anxiety first.

Depression about Hurt

Depression about hurt is provoked by the unhealthy belief 'I absolutely should not be feeling hurt' or 'I absolutely should not have been hurt again' or 'I absolutely should not have allowed myself to get hurt again', the fact that I did is awful, unbearable and proves I am a failure (or some other form of self damning belief). It is possible to have these three derivative beliefs or any combination of them. If you feel depressed about your hurt feelings then you will need to work through these feelings of depression as well as your feelings of hurt. You can refer back to Chapter 2 if you want to work on your feelings of depression first.

Anger about Hurt

Self anger about hurt is provoked by the unhealthy belief 'I absolutely should not be feeling hurt' or 'I absolutely should not have allowed myself to get hurt again', the fact that I did is awful, unbearable and proves I'm a weak person (or some other form of self damning belief). It is possible to have these three derivative beliefs or any combination of them. If you feel anger about your hurt feelings then you will need to work through these feelings of anger as well as your feelings of hurt. You can refer back to Chapter 3 if you want to work on your feelings of anger first.

Shame about Hurt

Feeling shame or embarrassment about your hurt feelings is provoked by the unhealthy belief 'People I know must not think I'm an idiot for feeling hurt' or 'People I know must not judge me negatively because I feel hurt again' or 'People I know must not judge me negatively because I've allowed myself to get hurt again', if they do it would be awful, unbearable and prove they are right that I am an idiot (or some other form of self damning belief). It is possible to have these three derivative beliefs or any combination of them. Shame and embarrassment are provoked by unhealthy beliefs that something shameful has been revealed about you. If you feel shame about your hurt feelings then you will need to work through these feelings of shame as well as your feelings of hurt. You can refer to Chapter 7 if you want to work on your feelings of shame first.

Common Hurt Triggers

The following are common triggers of hurt – it is not an exhaustive list. Tick the boxes that you think apply to you.

Tick the box to identify your hurt triggers

☐	Insulted	☐	Broken promise
☐	Offended	☐	Rejected
☐	Let down	☐	Excluded
☐	Betrayed	☐	Ignored
☐	Treated badly	☐	Lack of care
☐	Treated insensitively	☐	Lack of attention
☐	Not listened to	☐	Dismissed

☐ Not being number one in someone's mind
☐ Not being the most significant other with someone
☐ Tone of significant other's voice
☐ Lack of reciprocity

☐ Thoughtlessness
☐ Not treated in exactly the same way
☐ Other (write your own reason)

Am I Hurt or Disappointed?

At the heart of your hurt feelings are unhealthy beliefs about being treated badly, let down or betrayed by someone (and you think you do not deserve such treatment) and/or they are provoked by an unhealthy belief about someone who appears to hold your relationship less dearly than you thought. Unhealthy beliefs that provoke hurt have a consequence on how you think (cognitive consequences), act or tend to act (action tendencies). When you feel hurt, for example, your thoughts may be preoccupied with 'being treated badly' and how uncaring the other person has been. You may shut down all communication with the person responsible for your bad treatment or criticise them without telling them what you are feeling hurt about.

Assess if you are hurt or disappointed by checking your cognitive consequences and action tendencies.

Look through the illustrations for the cognitive consequences and action tendencies and work out if you are hurt or disappointed. It is important to put yourself in the trigger situation when you felt hurt. It is easy to think that you don't have unhealthy beliefs and thoughts when you are not triggered or when you are away from the person who triggered your hurt feelings. Imagine yourself with the person in question and imagine the moment when you felt the emotional pain. Work out if the pain was hurt or disappointment.

Cognitive Consequences

Hurt

You overestimate the unfairness of the other person's behaviour.

Cognitive Consequences

Disappointment

You are realistic about the unfairness of the other person's behaviour.

Cognitive Consequences

Hurt

You perceive others showing lack of care or indifference.

Cognitive Consequences

Disappointment

You perceive others as behaving badly rather than indifferent or uncaring.

Cognitive Consequences

Hurt

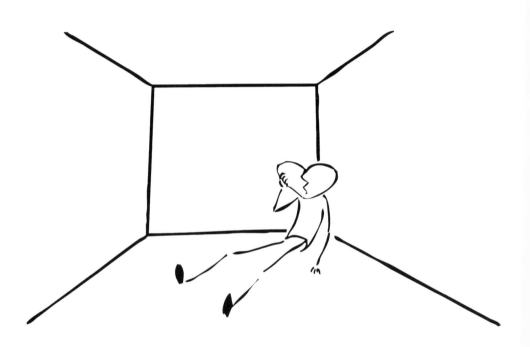

You see yourself as alone, uncared for and misunderstood.

Cognitive Consequences

Disappointment

You do not see yourself as alone or uncared for.

Cognitive Consequences

Hurt

You tend to think of past hurts.

Cognitive Consequences

Disappointment

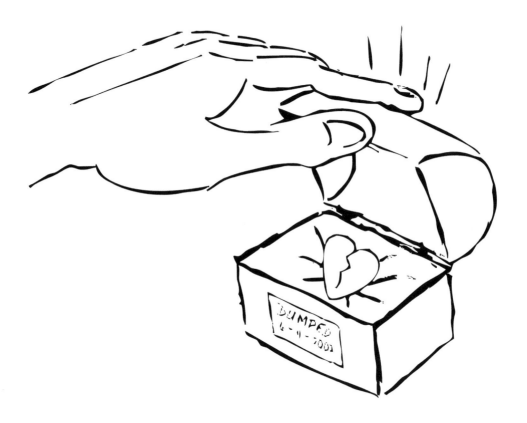

You are less likely to think of past hurts.

Cognitive Consequences

Hurt

You think the other has to put things right of their own accord first.

Cognitive Consequences

Disappointment

You do not think the other person has to make the first move.

Action/Action Tendencies

Hurt

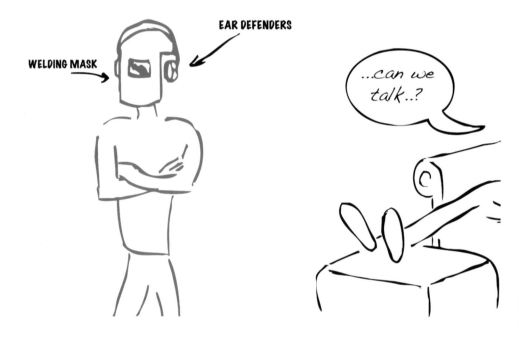

You shut down communication channels with the other person.

Action/Action Tendencies

Disappointment

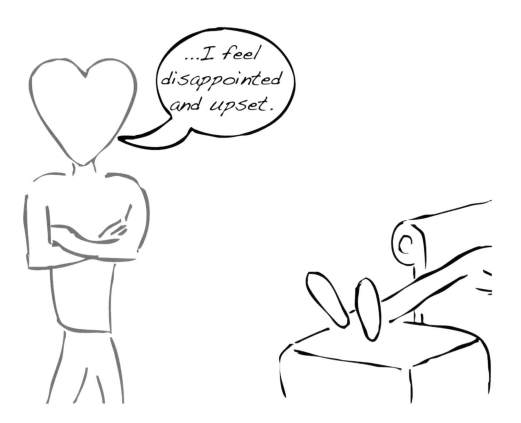

You are able to communicate your feelings to the other person directly.

You criticise the other person without disclosing what you are hurt about.

Disappointment

You influence the other person to act in a fairer manner.

Now . . .

General Change or Philosophical Change for you?

General Change

STEP 1   Choose a typical example of your hurt problem.

STEP 2   Identify your hurt cognitive consequences and action tendencies and write them in your own words, using the illustrations as a guide. Make sure that they are specific to your example.

STEP 3   Identify your disappointment cognitive consequences and action tendencies and write them in your own words, using the illustrations as a guide. Make sure they are specific to your example.

STEP 4   Commit to thinking and behaving in accordance with your healthy cognitive consequences and action tendencies for disappointment.

STEP 5   Repeat, Repeat, Repeat in a consistent and forceful manner until your new thinking and your new behaviour become second nature.

> **Tip:**
> If behaving in accordance with healthy disappointment is too overwhelming to begin with, then *imagine* yourself behaving in a healthy manner for a few weeks and then start in real life.

Philosophical Change

Remember to take time if you are choosing this route, as Philosophical Change is about changing your unhealthy beliefs over the long term.

STEP 1   Identify your unhealthy belief.

STEP 2   Dispute your unhealthy belief.

STEP 3   Identify your healthy belief.

STEP 4   Dispute your healthy belief.

STEP 5   Strengthen your healthy belief and weaken your unhealthy belief.

Remember, hurt is provoked by unhealthy beliefs about being treated badly, let down or betrayed by someone (and you think you do not deserve such treatment) and/or it is provoked by an unhealthy belief about someone who appears to hold your relationship less dearly than you thought.

An unhealthy belief is made up of absolutist **rigid beliefs** – MUSTs, HAVE TOs, NEED TOs, GOT TOs, ABSOLUTELY SHOULDs, from which three further derivative disturbed beliefs come.

AWFULISING BELIEF	LOW FRUSTRATION TOLERANCE BELIEF (LFT)	SELF DAMNING BELIEF
'It is awful.'	'I can't stand it.'	'I'm not good enough.'

A	B	→ C
Event or Trigger	**Belief**	**Consequences**
Most hurt	Rigid belief and its	Hurt
provoking event	derivatives	Cognitive Consequences
		Behaviour
		Action Tendencies
		Physical symptoms

A rigid belief, at **B**, is a demand about the most hurt provoking aspect of an event – it is either a demand about how you **absolutely should have been treated** or a demand about how you **absolutely should not have been treated.**

For example, if what you are most hurt about was being spoken to in an insensitive manner, then the rigid belief is **I should have been spoken to with respect** or **I absolutely should not have been spoken to in such an insensitive manner.**

The fact your rigid demand was not met triggers any or a combination of the three derivative beliefs.

RIGID BELIEF	AWFULISING BELIEF	LOW FRUSTRATION TOLERANCE BELIEF (LFT)	SELF DAMNING BELIEF
'I absolutely should have been spoken to with respect ...'	'... and it was awful that I was not spoken to with respect.'	'It is unbearable not to have been spoken to with respect.'	'The fact that I wasn't spoken to with respect proves I am worthless.'

Step 1

Identify your unhealthy hurt provoking belief

a. Choose a typical example of your hurt problem.

b. Use the previous Common Hurt Triggers table as a reference to pinpoint what you were most hurt about. You may have more than one trigger, which means you may have more than one hurt provoking belief. Work on one belief at a time.

c. Express your answer to Question (b) above in the form of an 'ABSOLUTE SHOULD'. (See previous examples.)

d. Identify the three derivative beliefs. (Awfulising, Low Frustration Tolerance (LFT), Self Damning. See page 5 as a reminder to what these mean.)

You may have all three derivatives or any combination of the three.

Remember to imagine yourself in the trigger situation when identifying these derivative beliefs.

Examples	A	LFT	SD/OD
'I absolutely should have been spoken to with respect by my friend. The fact that I wasn't is awful, unbearable and proves I'm worthless.'	✓	✓	✓
'I absolutely should be thought about first; I can't stand it when I am not and it means I am unlovable.'		✓	✓
'I absolutely should not be let down by my friend. The fact that I was is unbearable and proves I am worthless.'		✓	✓
'I absolutely should not have been betrayed by him; the fact that I was is terrible and I can't stand it and means I am unlovable.'	✓	✓	✓

Key: A = Awfulising, LFT = Low Frustration Tolerance, SD = Self Damning, OD = Other Damning

Step 2

dispute? your unhealthy h♥rt provoking belief

Question the validity of your unhealthy belief, using the following three criteria. Remember that an unhealthy belief is made up of the rigid belief and its derivatives. The disputing questions below are used on all of them.

a. Are they realistic or not and why?
b. Do they make sense or not and why?
c. Do they lead to helpful or unhelpful outcomes for me, and why?

Let's assume your unhealthy belief was as follows:

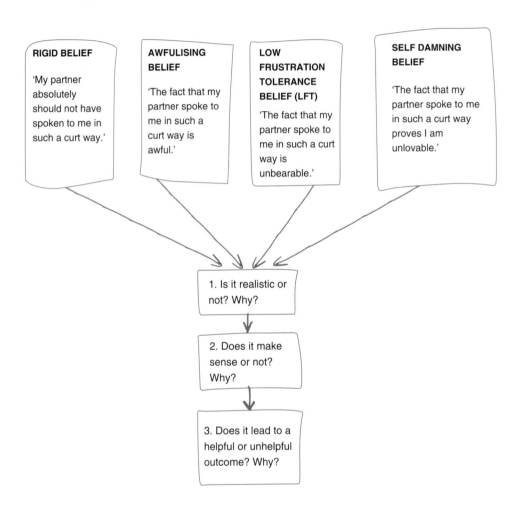

RIGID BELIEF

'My partner absolutely should not have spoken to me in such a curt way.'

AWFULISING BELIEF

'The fact that my partner spoke to me in such a curt way is awful.'

LOW FRUSTRATION TOLERANCE BELIEF (LFT)

'The fact that my partner spoke to me in such a curt way is unbearable.'

SELF DAMNING BELIEF

'The fact that my partner spoke to me in such a curt way proves I am unlovable.'

1. Is it realistic or not? Why?

2. Does it make sense or not? Why?

3. Does it lead to a helpful or unhelpful outcome? Why?

Go ahead and dispute your unhealthy belief or beliefs.

Step 3

identify your healthy disappointment provoking belief

a. Change your unhealthy belief and work out the healthy version by removing the rigidity and replacing it with the preference belief.

b. Remember to negate your unhealthy demand. For example, 'I would have liked my friend to have treated me with respect but it doesn't mean I absolutely should have been.'

c. Identify the derivative beliefs (Anti-awfulising, High Frustration Tolerance (HFT), Self/Other/World Acceptance. See page 7 as a reminder to what these mean.) Use the examples below as a guide.

d. Remember, preference beliefs are flexible, make sense and lead to a helpful outcome.

Unhealthy beliefs	A	LFT	SD/OD
'I absolutely should have been spoken to with respect by my friend. The fact that I wasn't is awful, unbearable and proves I'm worthless.'	✓	✓	✓
'I absolutely should be thought about first. I can't stand it and means I am unlovable.'		✓	✓
'I absolutely should not be let down by my friend. The fact that I was is unbearable and proves I am worthless.'		✓	✓
'I absolutely should not have been betrayed by him. The fact that I was is terrible, I can't stand it and it proves I am unlovable.'	✓	✓	✓

Healthy versions	AA	HFT	SA/OA
'I would have preferred to have been spoken to with respect by my friend but it doesn't mean that I absolutely should have been. The fact that I wasn't is bad but not awful, difficult but not unbearable, doesn't prove I'm worthless. I accept myself. I'm fallible like everyone else despite the fact I was spoken to disrespectfully.'	✓	✓	✓
'I strongly prefer to be thought about first but I do not have to be. It is uncomfortable but not unbearable and it does not prove I am unlovable. I accept myself as a fallible human being even when I am not thought about first.'		✓	✓
'I prefer not to be let down by my friend, but it doesn't mean that I mustn't be. The fact that I was let down is difficult but not unbearable and does not prove I am worthless. I accept myself despite being let down.'		✓	✓
'I prefer not to have been betrayed, but I accept that I was by him, but it doesn't mean that I absolutely shouldn't have been. The fact that I was is very bad but not terrible and doesn't prove I am unlovable. I accept myself regardless of the betrayal.'	✓		✓

Key: A = Awfulising, LFT = Low Frustration Tolerance, SD = Self Damning, OD = Other Damning, AA = Anti Awfulising, HFT = High Frustration Tolerance, SA = Self Acceptance, OA = Other Acceptance

Go ahead and rewrite your beliefs in a healthy way.

Step 4

dispute? your healthy disappointment provoking belief

Dispute your healthy beliefs using the same criteria used in disputing the unhealthy beliefs – this keeps it fair and you are more likely to persuade yourself to commit to changing them if you dispute the unhealthy and the healthy beliefs in exactly the same way.

Remember that a healthy belief is made up of a preference belief and its three balanced derivatives or a combination of them. The disputing questions below are used on all of them.

HEALTHY BELIEF

'I would have liked that my partner had spoken to me with respect but it doesn't mean he absolutely should have.'

ANTI-AWFULISING BELIEF

'The fact that my partner spoke to me disrespectfully is bad but not awful.'

HIGH FRUSTRATION TOLERANCE BELIEF (HFT)

'The fact that my partner spoke to me disrespectfully is difficult but bearable.'

SELF ACCEPTANCE BELIEF

'The fact that my partner spoke to me disrespectfully doesn't prove I'm unlovable. I accept myself unconditionally regardless.'

1. Is it realistic or not? Why?

2. Does it make sense or not? Why?

3. Does it lead to a helpful or unhelpful outcome? Why?

Tip:
Remember that anti-awfulising is where 100% bad does not exist, as one can usually think of something worse.

Tip:
HFT means you have not disintegrated.

Tip:
Self/other acceptance is not dependent on conditions. We are all fallible human beings.

Go ahead and dispute your healthy belief.

Step 5

STRENGTHEN your healthy disappointment provoking belief

weaken your unhealthy hurt provoking belief

In order to change your hurt provoking belief to a disappointment provoking one, you need to think in accordance with your healthy belief and take constructive actions. The illustrations demonstrate the thinking (cognitive consequences) and the action tendencies of disappointment. The constructive actions are based on the action tendencies of disappointment.

- Think and act in accordance with your healthy disappointment provoking belief repeatedly and consistently in a forceful manner until eventually your emotional state changes from hurt to disappointment.

- Remember your emotion of hurt **will** change – the new way of thinking and the new actions you will implement will feel uncomfortable initially but this is completely natural. You are changing an old habit of unhealthy thinking and old habitual hurt behaviours. It takes a few weeks of repetitions done consistently and forcefully.

- The behavioural goals you set for yourself need to be challenging but not overwhelming. If you overwhelm yourself then it defeats the object of the exercise.

- Start with imagining yourself thinking and acting in a healthy manner whilst being in the trigger situation until you think you are ready to challenge yourself in real life. For example, imagine yourself responding to your partner or friend by explaining that you feel disappointed about the way you have been treated and then asking them to treat you differently in the future.

- Repeat your healthy disappointment provoking belief in your head daily and particularly when you are imagining yourself in the trigger situation. This mental rehearsal will help you to remember it when you deliberately face the trigger situation in real life.

- Once you achieve your desired goal, whatever it is, then you need to maintain the helpful thinking and actions. For example, expressing your feelings in a balanced way rather than stopping communication altogether.

- Review how you did, each time you challenge yourself, and then work out what you can do differently or better the next time. Then do it. Do not demand perfection from yourself. The process of moving from hurt to disappointment is uncomfortable and uneven. Some days you will make bigger strides when you challenge yourself and other days you will make small strides or even take a step back. The important thing is to accept that this can happen and then bring your focus back to what you are doing and continue with it.

- Remember, you didn't learn to drive a car, ride a bicycle or learn to read overnight, it takes repetition and focus and consistency.

Chapter 5 – Hurt – Takeaway Tips

The following are some general helpful tips for any type of relationship:

- Accept that you are responsible for your own emotions and actions.

- Communicate without pointing a finger or without shutting down, use expressions like, 'I feel disappointed about the way you . . .' and not 'You caused me hurt . . .'

- Accept yourself as a valuable but imperfect human being, and think the same of your parents, relatives, brothers and sisters, friends and colleagues at work. Judge the way you have been treated rather than your worth.

- Be assertive and tell them about your hurt feelings, do not shut down communication with a significant other.

- Communicate your thoughts and feelings appropriately and not defensively. Being assertive means that you have the courage of your own convictions and that you can listen.

CHAPTER 6

Jealousy and Concern for One's Relationship

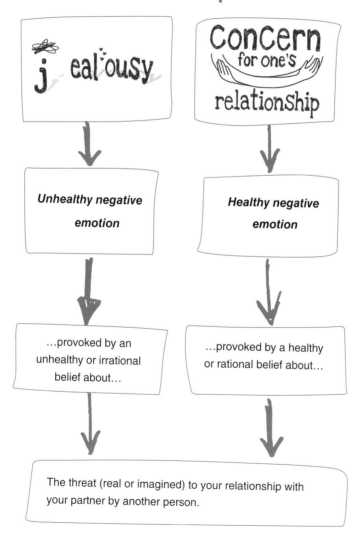

jealousy

concern for one's relationship

Unhealthy negative emotion

Healthy negative emotion

…provoked by an unhealthy or irrational belief about…

…provoked by a healthy or rational belief about…

The threat (real or imagined) to your relationship with your partner by another person.

Jealousy, in effect, involves three people so there is a triangular relationship and it is a defining characteristic of jealousy: the threat from someone else to your relationship with your partner. The words jealousy and envy are often mixed up. Envy is about someone possessing something or even someone YOU desire. In this chapter we will be looking at some of the most common triggers for jealousy.

Jealousy

Jealousy is a highly destructive emotion. It can lead to aggression and violence and sadly even loss of life. 'Crimes of passion' are, on the whole, fuelled by jealousy. Jealousy can trigger extreme anger and hostility when rigid unhealthy beliefs are held demanding that the other person MUST love only them forever.

Jealousy contaminates relationships like a virus. When you feel jealous, you tend to behave in a possessive manner, looking and finding signs of infidelity (or of love interest) by your partner. It is destructive because the pain and misery is not just felt by the sufferer of jealousy but by the partner too. If you feel jealous you tend to monitor and check your partner; checking text messages, emails, letters, aftershave/perfume, underwear, questioning your partner and so on. A lot of the time your mind is preoccupied with thoughts of infidelity, wondering if your partner is committing it or thinking about it. With the constant vigilance over your partner's behaviour, it is more than probable that you are also experiencing intense anxiety for much of the time. Even when you are in the company of your partner the vigilance is apparent, as you look for signs of the threat when out socialising together. You may remain preoccupied with it mentally even when you get home or you may start quizzing or accusing your partner.

When you experience jealousy it often tends to be accompanied by other unhealthy negative emotions of anxiety, anger, and self pity depression. If you experience these emotions alongside your jealous feelings then please refer to the chapters on anxiety (1), depression (2) and anger (3) to work through such problems too.

The following are typical jealousy provoking unhealthy beliefs:

- 'If my husband looks at another woman, which he must not do, it means that he finds her more attractive than me. This must not happen, but if it does it proves that I am worthless.'
- 'I absolutely have to know that my partner is interested in me and only me forever; the thought of my partner becoming interested in someone is unbearable and awful.'
- 'My partner must only find me attractive and must not leave me otherwise it proves I'm worthless.'
- 'My partner must only love me and never leave, otherwise he and the other person are worthless and bad people.'
- 'My partner is allowed to find other people attractive, but he/she must find me more attractive than anyone else otherwise I'm inadequate and not good enough.'
- 'I must be the only person my partner has ever been in love with; I can't bear that I might not be.'

If you experience jealousy you may hold a belief that you can only feel 'worthwhile' if you are the centre and object of your partner's love interest. This means that your worth is dependent on your partner's thoughts, feelings and behaviour towards you. Unfortunately, this is out of your control and it is important to care but not so that your life and worth depend on it.

Common Jealousy Triggers

The following are common themes of jealousy – the list is not exhaustive. Tick the boxes that you think apply to you.

Tick the box to identify your jealousy triggers

- ☐ Seeing your partner pay attention to someone else.
- ☐ Imagining your partner is seeing someone else.
- ☐ Partner's apparent lack of attention
- ☐ Partner not always at your side
- ☐ Imagining your partner is with the other person
- ☐ Imagining partner's emotional attachment with other person
- ☐ Checking /evaluating self against other members of the same sex
- ☐ Negative evaluation against other members of the same sex
- ☐ Imagining your partner is about to leave you for someone else
- ☐ Hearing your partner make positive comments about someone else
- ☐ Seeing your partner look at someone else
- ☐ Seeing your partner talk to someone
- ☐ Your partner's ex
- ☐ Your partner's past loves
- ☐ Your partner's friendship/s
- ☐ Your partner's work colleague/s
- ☐ Other (write your own reason)

Am I Jealous or Concerned for my Relationship?

At the heart of your jealousy are unhealthy rigid beliefs about a threat to your relationship with your partner from another person.

Such unhealthy beliefs not only provoke jealousy but they have a consequence on how you think (cognitive consequences), and what you feel like doing (action tendencies).

When you feel jealous, for example, your thoughts may be preoccupied with 'my partner will leave for someone else' and you may then seek constant assurance and reassurance.

Look through the illustrations for the cognitive consequences and action tendencies and work out if you are jealous or concerned for your relationship. It is important to put yourself in the trigger situation when you feel or felt jealous. It is easy to think that you don't have unhealthy rigid beliefs when you are not triggered or when you are away from the threat, so just imagine yourself in the frying pan, so to speak, and then work out if you are jealous or concerned for your relationship.

Cognitive Consequences

Jealousy

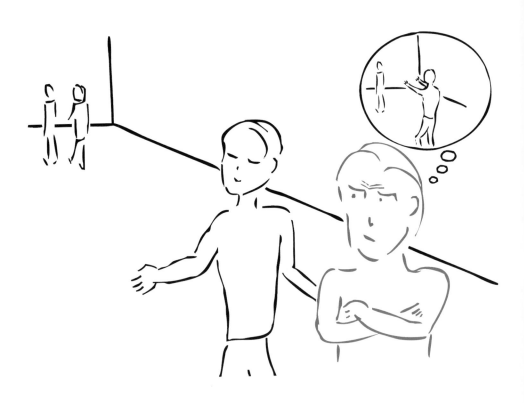

You tend to see a threat to your relationship when none exists.

Cognitive Consequences

Concern for One's Relationship

You tend not to see a threat to your relationship
when none exists.

Cognitive Consequences

Jealousy

You think the loss of your relationship is imminent.

Cognitive Consequences

Concern for One's Relationship

You do not think the loss of your relationship is imminent.

Jealousy

You tend to misconstrue your partner's ordinary conversations with another man or woman as having a romantic or sexual connotation.

Cognitive Consequences

Concern for One's Relationship

You do not misconstrue your partner's ordinary conversations with another man or woman as having a romantic or sexual connotation.

Cognitive Consequences

Jealousy

You construct visual images in your mind of your partner's infidelity.

Cognitive Consequences

Concern for One's Relationship

You do not construct visual images of your partner's infidelity.

Cognitive Consequences

Jealousy

If your partner admits to finding another person attractive you believe that the other is seen as more attractive than you and your partner will leave you for the other person.

Cognitive Consequences

Concern for One's Relationship

You accept your partner will find other people attractive but you do not see it as a threat.

You seek constant reassurance that you are loved.

Action/Action Tendencies

Concern for One's Relationship

You allow your partner to express their love without seeking
reassurance.

Jealousy

You monitor the reactions and feelings of your partner.

Action/Action Tendencies

Concern for One's Relationship

You allow your partner freedom without monitoring his or her feelings/actions and whereabouts.

You search for evidence that your partner is with someone else.

Action/Action Tendencies

Concern for One's Relationship

You allow your partner to show natural interest in other people without setting tests.

Jealousy

You attempt to restrict the movements or activities of your partner.

Action/Action Tendencies

Concern for One's Relationship

You do not restrict the movements or activities of your partner.

You set tests which your partner has to pass.

Action/Action Tendencies

Concern for One's Relationship

You do not set tests.

Jealousy

You retaliate for your partner's 'presumed' infidelity.

Action/Action Tendencies

Concern for One's Relationship

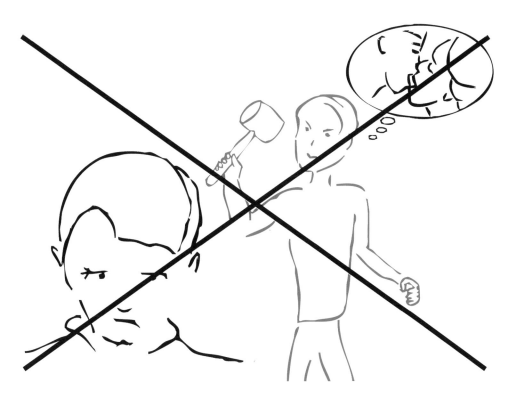

You do not retaliate for your partner's 'presumed' infidelity.

You sulk.

Action/Action Tendencies

Concern for One's Relationship

You don't sulk.

Now . . .

General Change or Philosophical Change for you?

General Change

STEP 1   Choose a typical example of your jealousy.

STEP 2   Identify your jealousy cognitive consequences and action tendencies and write them in your own words, using the illustrations as a guide. Make sure that they are specific to your example.

STEP 3   Identify your concern for your relationship cognitive consequences and action tendencies and write them in your own words, using the illustrations as a guide. Make sure they are specific to your example.

STEP 4   Commit to thinking and behaving in accordance with your healthy cognitive consequences and action tendencies for concern for your relationship.

STEP 5   Repeat, Repeat, Repeat in a consistent and forceful manner until your new thinking and your new behaviour become second nature.

> **Tip:**
> If behaving in accordance with concern for your relationship is too overwhelming to begin with, then *imagine* yourself behaving in a healthy manner for a few weeks and then start in real life.

Philosophical Change

Remember to take your time if you are choosing this route, as Philosophical Change is about changing your unhealthy beliefs over the long term.

STEP 1   Identify your unhealthy belief.

STEP 2   Dispute your unhealthy belief.

STEP 3   Identify your healthy belief.

STEP 4   Dispute your healthy belief.

STEP 5   Strengthen your healthy belief and weaken your unhealthy belief.

Remember, jealousy is provoked by unhealthy beliefs about a threat to your relationship with your partner from another person. Unhealthy beliefs are made up of absolutist **rigid beliefs** in the form of a MUST, HAVE TO, NEED TO, GOT TO, ABSOLUTELY SHOULD, from which three further derivative beliefs come.

AWFULISING BELIEF	LOW FRUSTRATION TOLERANCE BELIEF (LFT)	SELF DAMNING BELIEF
'It would be awful.'	'It would be unbearable.'	'I am inadequate and worthless.'

A	**B** $\longrightarrow$	**C**
Event or Trigger	**Belief**	**Consequences**
Most jealousy provoking event	Rigid belief and its derivatives	Jealousy
		Cognitive Consequences
		Behaviour
		Action Tendencies
		Physical symptoms

A rigid belief, at **B**, is a demand about the most jealousy provoking aspect of an event – it is either a demand for it to **absolutely happen** or **absolutely not happen.**

For example, if what you are jealous about is your partner's previous relationships, then the rigid belief may be '**My partner must love me more than anyone else**', or '**I must be the only one he has ever loved**'. If what you are most jealous about is your partner leaving you for someone else, then your rigid belief is '**My partner must never leave me for someone else**'. The consequence of not having the rigid belief met is any or a combination of the three derivative beliefs.

For example:

RIGID BELIEF	AWFULISING BELIEF	LOW FRUSTRATION TOLERANCE BELIEF (LFT)	SELF DAMNING BELIEF
'My partner must never leave me for someone else.'	'If my partner left me for someone else it would be awful.'	'If my partner left me for someone else it would be unbearable.'	'If my partner left me for someone else it would prove I am worthless.'

Step 1

Identify your unhealthy jealousy provoking belief

a. Choose a typical example of your jealousy problem.

b. Use the previous Common Jealousy Triggers table as a reference to pinpoint what you were most jealous about. You may have more than one trigger, which means you may have more than one jealousy provoking belief. Work on one belief at a time.

c. Express your answer to Question (b) above in the form of a 'MUST' or 'MUST NOT'. (See previous examples.)

d. Identify the three derivative beliefs. (Awfulising, Low Frustration Tolerance (LFT), Self Damning. See page 5 as a reminder to what these mean.)

You may have all three derivatives or any combination of the three.

Remember to imagine yourself in the trigger situation when identifying these derivative beliefs.

Examples	A	LFT	SD/OD
'I must be loved more than anyone else by my partner; I can't stand it if I am not.'		✓	
'My partner must never leave me for someone else. It would be awful and unbearable and would prove I am worthless.'	✓	✓	✓
'My partner must only be interested in me and only me. If he isn't it would be awful and unbearable.'	✓	✓	
'My partner must only find me attractive. If he doesn't it would be awful, unbearable and proves I'm worthless.'	✓	✓	✓

Key: A = Awfulising, LFT = Low Frustration Tolerance, SD = Self Damning, OD = Other Damning

Step 2

dispute? your unhealthy jealousy provoking belief

Question the validity of your unhealthy belief, using the following three criteria. Remember that an unhealthy belief is made up of the rigid belief and its derivatives. The disputing questions below are used on all of them.

a. Are they realistic or not and why?
b. Do they make sense or not and why?
c. Do they lead to helpful or unhelpful outcomes for me, and why?

Let's assume your unhealthy belief was as follows:

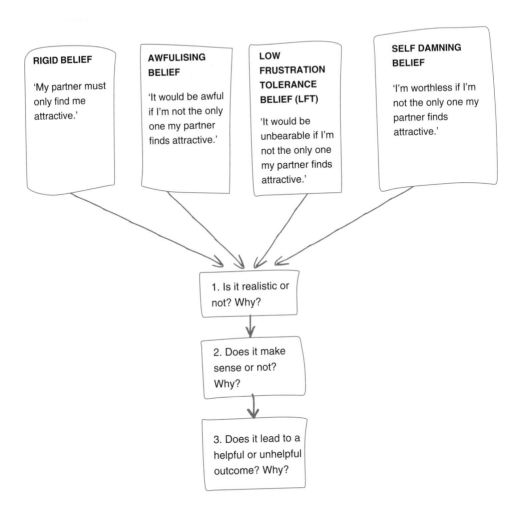

RIGID BELIEF

'My partner must only find me attractive.'

AWFULISING BELIEF

'It would be awful if I'm not the only one my partner finds attractive.'

LOW FRUSTRATION TOLERANCE BELIEF (LFT)

'It would be unbearable if I'm not the only one my partner finds attractive.'

SELF DAMNING BELIEF

'I'm worthless if I'm not the only one my partner finds attractive.'

1. Is it realistic or not? Why?

2. Does it make sense or not? Why?

3. Does it lead to a helpful or unhelpful outcome? Why?

Go ahead and dispute your unhealthy belief or beliefs.

Step 3

identify your healthy concern for one's relationship provoking belief

a. Change your unhealthy belief and work out the healthy version by removing the rigidity and replacing it with the preference belief.

b. Remember to negate your unhealthy demand. For example, 'I'd prefer to be the only one my partner finds attractive BUT I do not absolutely have to be'.

c. Identify the derivative beliefs (Anti-awfulising, High Frustration Tolerance (HFT), Self/Other/World Acceptance. See page 7 as a reminder to what these mean.) Use the examples below as a guide.

d. Remember, preference beliefs are flexible, make sense and lead to a helpful outcome.

Unhealthy beliefs	A	LFT	SD/OD
'I must be loved more than anyone else by my partner; I can't stand it if I am not.'		✓	
'My partner must never leave me for someone else, it would be awful and unbearable and would prove I am worthless.'	✓	✓	✓
'My partner must be interested in me and only me. If he isn't it would be awful and unbearable.'	✓	✓	✓
'My partner must only find me attractive. If he doesn't it is awful, unbearable and proves I'm worthless.'			✓

Healthy versions	AA	HFT	SA/OA
'I'd like to be loved more than anyone else by my partner but it doesn't mean I absolutely must be. It would be difficult but I will stand it.'		✓	
'I want my partner to never leave me for someone else, but it doesn't mean that he absolutely mustn't. If he does it would be very difficult but I can bear it; it doesn't mean I am worthless. I'm fallible. I accept myself regardless.'		✓	✓
'I prefer that he is interested in me and only me but it doesn't mean he absolutely must be. If he becomes interested in someone else that would be very bad but not the end of the world for me. It would be very difficult but I would survive.'	✓	✓	
'I want my partner to only find me attractive but it doesn't mean he has to. If not it would be bad but not awful, difficult but bearable. It doesn't mean I am worthless. I am fallible and accept myself regardless.'	✓	✓	✓

Key: A = Awfulising, LFT = Low Frustration Tolerance, SD = Self Damning, OD = Other Damning, AA = Anti Awfulising, HFT = High Frustration Tolerance, SA = Self Acceptance, OA = Other Acceptance

Go ahead and rewrite your beliefs in a healthy way.

Step 4

Dispute your healthy beliefs using the same criteria used in disputing the unhealthy beliefs – this keeps it fair and you are more likely to persuade yourself to commit to changing them if you dispute the unhealthy and the healthy beliefs in exactly the same way.

Remember that a healthy belief is made up of a preference belief and its three balanced derivatives or a combination of them. The disputing questions below are used on all of them.

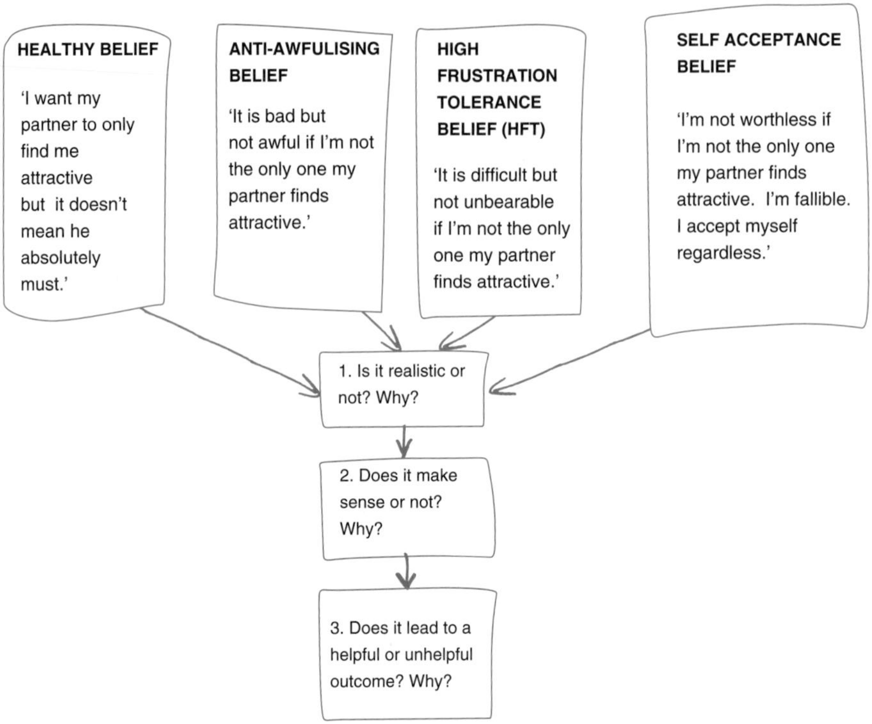

HEALTHY BELIEF

'I want my partner to only find me attractive but it doesn't mean he absolutely must.'

ANTI-AWFULISING BELIEF

'It is bad but not awful if I'm not the only one my partner finds attractive.'

HIGH FRUSTRATION TOLERANCE BELIEF (HFT)

'It is difficult but not unbearable if I'm not the only one my partner finds attractive.'

SELF ACCEPTANCE BELIEF

'I'm not worthless if I'm not the only one my partner finds attractive. I'm fallible. I accept myself regardless.'

1. Is it realistic or not? Why?

2. Does it make sense or not? Why?

3. Does it lead to a helpful or unhelpful outcome? Why?

Tip:
Remember that anti-awfulising is where 100% bad does not exist, as one can usually think of something worse.

Tip:
HFT means you have not disintegrated.

Tip:
Self/other acceptance is not dependent on conditions. We are all fallible human beings.

Go ahead and dispute your healthy belief and its balanced derivatives.

Step 5

weaken your unhealthy jealousy provoking belief

In order to change your jealousy provoking belief to a concern for your relationship provoking one, you need to think in accordance with your healthy belief and take constructive actions. The illustrations demonstrate the thinking (cognitive consequences) and action tendencies of concern for your relationship. The constructive actions are based on the action tendencies of concern for your relationship.

- Think and act in accordance with your healthy belief repeatedly and consistently in a forceful manner until eventually your emotional state changes from jealousy to concern.

- Remember your emotion of jealousy **will** change – the new way of thinking and the new actions you will implement will feel uncomfortable initially but this is completely natural. You are changing an old habit of unhealthy thinking and old habitual jealousy behaviours. It takes a few weeks of repetitions done consistently and forcefully.

- The behavioural goals you set for yourself need to be challenging but not overwhelming. If you overwhelm yourself then it defeats the object of the exercise.

- Start with imagining yourself thinking and acting in a healthy manner whilst being in the trigger situation until you think you are ready to challenge yourself in real life. For example, imagine yourself going out with your partner and not checking your partner's behaviour towards others, but at some point you will need to take action and go out with your partner and practise your new healthy belief in the situation then continue until you achieve your desired goal.

- Repeat your healthy belief in your head daily and particularly when you are imagining yourself in the trigger situation. This mental rehearsal will help you to remember it when you deliberately face the trigger situation in real life.

- Once you achieve your desired goal, whatever it is, then you need to maintain the helpful thinking and actions. For example, your goal may be to go out with your partner and enjoy the experience without checking your partner's behaviour towards others.

- Review how you did, each time you challenge yourself, and then work out what you can do differently or better the next time. Then do it. Do not demand perfection from yourself. The process of moving from jealousy to concern for your relationship is uncomfortable and uneven. Some days you will make bigger strides when you challenge yourself and other days you will make small strides or even take a step back. The important thing is to accept that this can happen and then bring your focus back to what you are doing and continue with it.

- Remember, you didn't learn to drive a car, ride a bicycle or learn to read overnight, it takes repetition and focus and consistency.

Chapter 6 – Jealousy – Takeaway Tips

- Be mindful of suggestions like 'how to make your partner addicted to you'. It's not healthy or realistic.

- Accept the things that are within your control and the things that are not. You can control what you believe and what you do. You are not in control of what your partner thinks, feels, imagines or does.

- Accept yourself unconditionally. Your worth does not depend on anyone or on anything.

- Involve yourself in activities that you enjoy and build your own pleasure in life rather than making your life about your partner.

CHAPTER 7

Shame and Regret

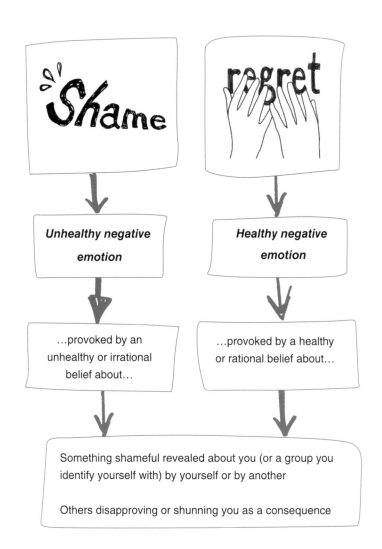

Shame and Embarrassment

Shame and embarrassment are feelings that are often experienced when there is either a real or a perceived public incident of some social gaffe. Both shame and embarrassment are provoked by unhealthy beliefs where you link your sense of worth to other people's negative judgement.

You find yourself agreeing with the way you think other people will judge you for the social gaffe or faux pas. The unhealthy belief is often as follows:

'Others must not disapprove of me for (whatever negative thing has been revealed about me), *because if they do and then judge me as weak, inept, incompetent, a failure, worthless etc, they'd be right.'*

We have worked with clients who also view the real or perceived social disapproval as the end of the world and as something intolerable. Almost all have had the self damning belief though.

Shame and embarrassment can trigger different physical symptoms and behaviours such as blushing, confusion, downward cast eyes, slack posture, lowered head, biting of lips or tongue, forced smile, fidgeting, being lost for words or having a blank mind.

Difference between Shame and Embarrassment

Shame and embarrassment are experienced about the same event, i.e. something negative has been revealed about me. The difference between them is that with shame, what's been revealed is far more serious than with embarrassment as far as you're concerned. It is subjective but we can all think of events that we would judge as embarrassing and events we would label as shameful. The roots of the word *shame* are thought to derive from an older word meaning 'to cover'; as such, covering oneself, literally or figuratively. Embarrassment and shame can be experienced by a person even if it's not specifically about that individual but about a group with which that individual identifies. For example, some cultures or some families within that culture perceive that they must rigidly adhere to certain behavioural rules and codes. Breaking such rules has resulted in aggressive, dangerous responses and sadly, in some cases, even murder. The person who has committed the shameful act is believed to be the 'cause' of the feeling of shame experienced by others as well as the 'cause' of the perceived shunning. As a consequence of this, anger and rage are provoked as a direct result of holding unhealthy beliefs about the person who has 'caused' the problem. It is not the person who has committed the 'shameful' act but the unhealthy beliefs others hold about it and about that individual that provoked feelings of shame and then anger.

Shame and Guilt

Shame and guilt are often misinterpreted or thought of as being the same. The focus of the shame provoking belief is other people's disapproval, whereas the focus of the guilt provoking belief is one's own disapproval of one's self for having broken one's own moral code.

Meta-Emotions of Shame and Embarrassment

A meta-emotion is an emotional problem about an emotional problem. For example, you can feel shame about feeling shame, depressed about feeling shame, angry about feeling shame and so on. You will know if you have a meta-emotion about your shame or embarrassment by asking yourself 'how do I feel about my shame and embarrassment feelings?'

If you have a meta-emotion about your shame and embarrassment feelings then go to the relevant chapter for that particular emotion and work through it.

Common Shame and Embarrassment Triggers

The following are common themes of shame and embarrassment – the list is not exhaustive. Tick the boxes that you think apply to you.

Tick the box to identify your shame and embarrassment triggers

- ☐ Looking anxious
- ☐ Showing any symptoms of anxiety
- ☐ Blushing
- ☐ Sweating of head, face, armpits or hands
- ☐ Stuttering
- ☐ Forgetting
- ☐ Making mistakes
- ☐ Not knowing something when asked
- ☐ Mind going blank
- ☐ Soiling yourself in public
- ☐ Wetting yourself in public
- ☐ Having an anxiety attack or a panic attack
- ☐ Loss of control
- ☐ Being annoyed or angry
- ☐ Looking emotional
- ☐ Acting emotionally
- ☐ Asking for more intimacy from partner
- ☐ Approaching partner for intimacy
- ☐ Talking to partner about sex
- ☐ Talking about sex

- ☐ Experiencing rejection
- ☐ Being laughed at
- ☐ Being the butt of someone's joke
- ☐ Being criticised
- ☐ Acting stupidly
- ☐ Being defeated
- ☐ Failing
- ☐ Being different
- ☐ Having a mental or emotional problem
- ☐ Having surgery
- ☐ Being ill/throwing up in public
- ☐ Losing some ability
- ☐ Lacking some ability
- ☐ Physical appearance
- ☐ Body shape and size
- ☐ Specific body part
- ☐ Sexual performance
- ☐ Sexual orientation
- ☐ Sexual desires
- ☐ Sexual pleasure
- ☐ Fainting in public
- ☐ Other (write your own reason)

Am I Feeling Shame/Embarrassment or Regret?

At the heart of your shame/embarrassment feelings are unhealthy beliefs about being disapproved of by others for having committed some socially unacceptable behaviour, the consequences of which are negative judgement and rejection. Unhealthy beliefs that provoke shame/embarrassment impact on the way you think (cognitive consequences), act or tend to act (action tendencies).

When you feel shame/embarrassment, for example, your thoughts may be preoccupied with how others are judging you, thinking that you are incompetent and that they are right for thinking that way about you. You may avoid and remove yourself from that situation and that group of people. Assess if you are feeling shame/embarrassment or regret by checking your thoughts, actions and action tendencies.

Look through the illustrations for the cognitive consequences and actions/action tendencies and work out if you are feeling shame/embarrassment or regret. It is important to put yourself in the trigger situation when you felt uncomfortable. It is easy to think that you don't have unhealthy thoughts when you are not triggered or when you are away from the trigger situation. Imagine yourself in the situation that triggered your feelings. Work out if the discomfort was shame/embarrassment or regret.

Cognitive Consequences

Shame/Embarrassment

You overestimate the shamefulness of the information revealed.

Cognitive Consequences

Regret

You see the information revealed in a compassionate, self accepting context.

Cognitive Consequences

Shame/Embarrassment

You overestimate the likelihood that the judging group will notice or be interested in the information.

Cognitive Consequences

Regret

You are realistic about the likelihood that the judging group will notice or be interested in the information.

You overestimate the degree of disapproval you will receive.

Cognitive Consequences

Regret

You are realistic about the degree of disapproval you
will receive.

You overestimate the length of time the disapproval
will last for.

Cognitive Consequences

Regret

You are realistic about the length of time the disapproval
will last for.

You remove yourself from the gaze of others.

Regret

You continue to participate actively in social interactions.

Shame/Embarrassment

You isolate yourself from other people.

Regret

You respond to attempts of others to restore the social equilibrium.

Shame/Embarrassment

You save face by attacking others who have shamed you.

Regret

You do not save face by attacking others.

You defend your threatened self esteem in self defeating ways.

Action/Action Tendencies

Regret

You do not defend your self esteem as it is not threatened.

You ignore attempts by others to restore social equilibrium.

Action/Action Tendencies

Regret

You do not ignore attempts by others to restore social equilibrium.

Now . . .

General Change or Philosophical Change for you?

General Change

STEP 1   Choose a typical example of your shame/embarrassment problem.

STEP 2   Identify your shame/embarrassment cognitive consequences and action tendencies and write them in your own words, using the illustrations as a guide. Make sure that they are specific to your example.

STEP 3   Identify your regret cognitive consequences and action tendencies and write them in your own words, using the illustrations as a guide. Make sure they are specific to your example.

STEP 4   Commit to thinking and behaving in accordance with your healthy cognitive consequences and action tendencies for regret.

STEP 5   Repeat, Repeat, Repeat in a consistent and forceful manner until your new thinking and your new behaviour become second nature.

Tip:
If behaving in accordance with healthy regret is too overwhelming to begin with, then *imagine* yourself behaving in a healthy manner for a few weeks and then start in real life.

Philosophical Change

Remember to take your time if you are choosing this route, as Philosophical Change is about changing your unhealthy beliefs over the long term.

STEP 1   Identify your unhealthy belief.

STEP 2   Dispute your unhealthy belief.

STEP 3   Identify your healthy belief.

STEP 4   Dispute your healthy belief.

STEP 5   Strengthen your healthy belief and weaken your unhealthy belief.

Remember, shame/embarrassment is provoked by unhealthy beliefs about being disapproved of by others for having committed some socially unacceptable behaviour, the consequences of which are negative judgement and rejection. An unhealthy belief is made up of absolutist **rigid beliefs** – MUSTs, HAVE TOs, NEED TOs, GOT TOs, ABSOLUTELY SHOULDs, from which three further derivative beliefs come.

AWFULISING BELIEF	LOW FRUSTRATION TOLERANCE BELIEF (LFT)	SELF DAMNING BELIEF
'It would be awful.'	'It would be unbearable.'	'It would mean I am bad.'

A

Event or Trigger

Shame/embarrassment

provoking event

B

Belief

Rigid belief and its

derivatives

C

Consequences

Shame/Embarrassment

Cognitive Consequences

Action Tendencies

Behaviour

Physical symptoms

A rigid belief, at **B**, is a demand about the most shame/embarrassment provoking aspect of an event – it is a demand about how **others must not disapprove of me for what has been revealed about me.**

For example, if what you are most embarrassed about is your family finding out that you secretly binge, the rigid belief will be **my family must not disapprove of me for secretly binging.**

The fact that your rigid demand was not met triggers any or a combination of the three derivative beliefs.

For example:

RIGID BELIEF	AWFULISING BELIEF	LOW FRUSTRATION TOLERANCE BELIEF (LFT)	SELF DAMNING BELIEF
'My family must not disapprove of me if they find out that I secretly binge.'	'If they do it would be awful.'	'If they do it would be unbearable.'	'If they do it proves I am a disgusting person.'

Step 1

Identify your unhealthy "Shame provoking belief

a. Choose a typical example of your shame/embarrassment problem.

b. Use the previous Common Shame/Embarrassment Triggers table as a reference to pinpoint what you were ashamed or embarrassed about. You may have more than one trigger, which means you may have more than one shame/embarrassment provoking belief. Work on one belief at a time.

c. Express your answer to Question (b) above in the form of a 'MUST'. (See above examples.)

d. Identify the derivative beliefs. (Awfulising, Low Frustration Tolerance (LFT), Self Damning. See page 5 as a reminder to what these mean.)

You may have all three derivatives or any combination of the three.

Remember to imagine yourself in the trigger situation when identifying these derivative beliefs.

Examples	A	LFT	SD/OD
'I must not be judged as weak because I blushed, because being judged as weak is awful, unbearable and proves that I'm weak.'	✓	✓	✓
'I must not be thought of as lightweight by my colleagues because I was sweating during a presentation. Being judged as lightweight proves that I am.'			✓
'My partner must not think I'm abnormal because I wanted to talk about sex. Being thought of as abnormal is unbearable.'		✓	
'My family must not think I am disgusting if they find out I secretly binge, if they do it would be awful and unbearable and prove I am disgusting.'	✓	✓	✓

Key: A = Awfulising, LFT = Low Frustration Tolerance, SD = Self Damning,
OD = Other Damning

Step 2

dispute? your unhealthy Shame provoking belief

Question the validity of your unhealthy belief, using the following three criteria. Remember that an unhealthy belief is made up of the rigid belief and its derivatives. The disputing questions below are used on all of them.

a. Are they realistic or not and why?
b. Do they make sense or not and why?
c. Do they lead to helpful or unhelpful outcomes for me, and why?

Let's assume your unhealthy belief was as follows:

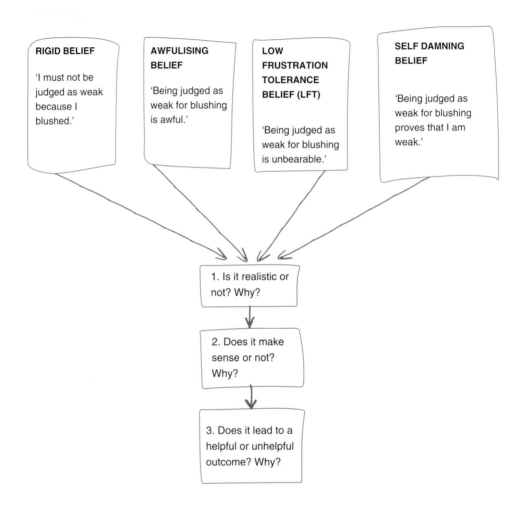

RIGID BELIEF

'I must not be judged as weak because I blushed.'

AWFULISING BELIEF

'Being judged as weak for blushing is awful.'

LOW FRUSTRATION TOLERANCE BELIEF (LFT)

'Being judged as weak for blushing is unbearable.'

SELF DAMNING BELIEF

'Being judged as weak for blushing proves that I am weak.'

1. Is it realistic or not? Why?

2. Does it make sense or not? Why?

3. Does it lead to a helpful or unhelpful outcome? Why?

Go ahead and dispute your unhealthy belief or beliefs.

Step 3

Identify your healthy regret provoking belief

a. Change your unhealthy belief and work out the healthy version by removing the rigidity and replacing it with the preference belief.

b. Remember to negate your unhealthy demand. For example, 'I'd like people not to judge me as weak because I blushed BUT it doesn't mean they mustn't'.

c. Identify the derivative beliefs (Anti-awfulising, High Frustration Tolerance (HFT), Self/Other/World Acceptance. See page 7 as a reminder to what these mean.) Use the examples below as a guide.

d. Remember, preference beliefs are flexible, make sense and lead to a helpful outcome.

Unhealthy beliefs	A	LFT	SD/OD
'I must not be judged as weak because I blushed, because being judged as weak is awful, unbearable and proves that I'm weak.'	✓	✓	✓
'I must not be thought of as lightweight by my colleagues because I was sweating during a presentation. Being judged as lightweight proves that I am.'			✓
'My partner must not think I'm abnormal because I wanted to talk about sex. Being thought of as abnormal is unbearable'.	✓	✓	✓
'My family must not think I am disgusting if they find out I secretly binge, if they do it would be awful and unbearable and prove I am disgusting.'		✓	

Healthy versions	AA	HFT	SA/OA
'I'd like people not to judge me as weak because I blushed but it doesn't mean that it mustn't happen. If I am it is bad but not awful, difficult but not unbearable; it doesn't prove that I'm weak, I'm fallible. I accept myself regardless of other people's judgement.'	✓	✓	✓
'I hope that my colleagues do not judge me as lightweight because I was sweating during a presentation, but it doesn't mean that they mustn't. If they do it doesn't mean that I am lightweight. I'm fallible, I accept myself regardless.'			✓
'I'd rather that my partner did not judge me as abnormal because I wanted to talk about sex but it doesn't mean she mustn't. If she does it would be difficult but not unbearable.'	✓	✓	✓
'I hope my family do not think I am disgusting because of my secret binging, but it doesn't mean that they mustn't. If they do it would be bad but not awful, difficult but bearable. It wouldn't mean that I am disgusting. I am a fallible person and I accept myself regardless.'		✓	

Key: A = Awfulising, LFT = Low Frustration Tolerance, SD = Self Damning, OD = Other Damning, AA = Anti Awfulising, HFT = High Frustration Tolerance, SA = Self Acceptance, OA = Other Acceptance

Go ahead and rewrite your beliefs in a healthy way.

Step 4

dispute? your

healthy regret

provoking belief

Dispute your healthy beliefs using the same criteria used in disputing the unhealthy beliefs – this keeps it fair and you are more likely to persuade yourself to commit to changing them if you dispute the unhealthy and the healthy beliefs in exactly the same way.

Remember that a healthy belief is made up of a preference belief and its three balanced derivatives or a combination of them. The disputing questions below are used on all of them.

HEALTHY BELIEF

'I'd like people not to judge me as weak because I blushed but it doesn't mean that it mustn't happen.'

ANTI-AWFULISING BELIEF

'Being judged as weak because of blushing is bad but not awful.'

HIGH FRUSTRATION TOLERANCE BELIEF (HFT)

'Being judged as weak for blushing is difficult but not unbearable.'

SELF ACCEPTANCE BELIEF

'Being judged as weak for blushing doesn't prove that I'm weak. I'm fallible. I accept myself regardless.'

1. Is it realistic or not? Why?

2. Does it make sense or not? Why?

3. Does it lead to a helpful or unhelpful outcome? Why?

Tip:
Remember that anti-awfulising is where 100% bad does not exist, as one can usually think of something worse.

Tip:
HFT means you have not disintegrated.

Tip:
Self/other acceptance is not dependent on conditions. We are all fallible human beings.

Go ahead and dispute your healthy belief and its balanced derivatives.

Step 5

STRENGTHEN your healthy regret provoking belief

weaken your unhealthy shame provoking belief

In order to change your shame/embarrassment provoking belief to a regret provoking one, you need to think in accordance with your healthy belief and take constructive actions. The illustrations demonstrate the thinking (cognitive consequences) and the action and action tendencies of regret. The constructive actions are based on the action tendencies of regret.

- Think and act in accordance with your healthy belief repeatedly and consistently in a forceful manner until eventually your emotional state changes from shame/embarrassment to a healthier one of regret.

- Remember your emotion of shame/embarrassment **will** change – the new way of thinking and the new actions you will implement will feel uncomfortable initially but this is completely natural. You are changing an old habit of unhealthy thinking and old habitual shame/embarrassment behaviours. It takes a few weeks of repetitions done consistently and forcefully.

- The behavioural goals you set for yourself need to be challenging but not overwhelming. If you overwhelm yourself then it defeats the object of the exercise.

- Start with imagining yourself thinking and acting in a healthy manner whilst being in the trigger situation until you think you are ready to challenge yourself in real life. For example, imagine yourself talking to your partner about sex whilst reciting your healthy belief in your head.

- Repeat your healthy belief in your head daily and particularly when you are imagining yourself in the trigger situation. This mental rehearsal will help you to remember it when you deliberately face the trigger situation in real life.

- Once you achieve your desired goal, whatever it is, then you need to maintain the helpful thinking and actions. For example, continue to challenge yourself by putting yourself in situations where it's possible to experience negative judgement

- Review how you did, each time you challenge yourself, and then work out what you can do differently or better the next time. Then do it. Do not demand perfection from yourself. The process of moving from shame/embarrassment to regret is uncomfortable and uneven. Some days you will make bigger strides when you challenge yourself and other days you will make small strides or even take a step back. The important thing is to accept that this can happen and then bring your focus back to what you are doing and continue with it.

- Remember, you didn't learn to drive a car, ride a bicycle or learn to read overnight, it takes repetition and focus and consistency.

Chapter 7 – Shame – Takeaway Tips

Shame Attacking Exercises

If you really want to free yourself from the grips of shame/embarrassment and learn to accept yourself unconditionally as a fallible human being regardless of other people's disapproval then you can engage in **shame attack**.

Shame attacking exercises involve you doing something that you would find shameful or embarrassing and then thinking in accordance with your healthy belief.

The following are examples of clients who committed to and engaged in shame attacking:

Example 1

The client was most anxious about the thought of fainting in a busy train carriage because the idea of other people's judgement as 'this person is odd and abnormal' felt embarrassing. The shame attacking exercise involved the client pretending to faint by dropping to the floor in the carriage of the busy train and lying there whilst reciting 'I really hope people are not judging me as abnormal for fainting but it doesn't mean they mustn't. If they do, it wouldn't mean that I'm abnormal, I accept myself regardless.'

This was carried out a few times and each time the client ended up with a seat and some warm attention from some but not from everyone. Eventually, the client accepted that some people may judge you, others may be indifferent and some show concern for your well-being.

Example 2

A client had anxiety about vomiting in public. The thought of others being repulsed by him triggered intense embarrassment. He agreed to pretend to throw up in a carrier bag whilst sitting on the bus. The client reported that some people moved away, some people were indifferent and a few came over and checked that he was OK. He was reciting his healthy belief before, during and after the exercise.

CHAPTER 8

Envy and Healthy Envy

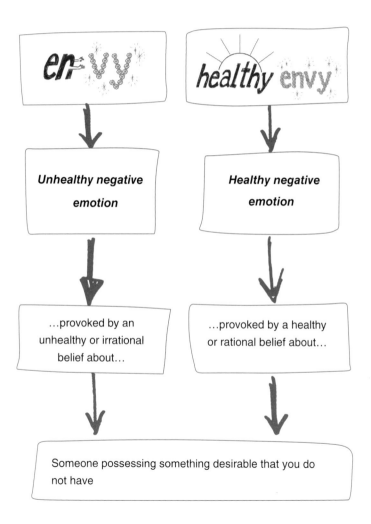

envy

↓

Unhealthy negative emotion

↓

...provoked by an unhealthy or irrational belief about...

healthy envy

↓

Healthy negative emotion

↓

...provoked by a healthy or rational belief about...

↓   ↓

Someone possessing something desirable that you do not have

Envy may involve wanting the beauty, wealth, abilities or socio-economic status of another individual or group. Envy, historically, is one of the seven deadly sins and is also often known as the 'evil eye' when what you have is envied by someone else. Thomas Aquinas wrote:

'Charity rejoices in our neighbour's good, while envy grieves over it.'

Unhealthy Envy

Unhealthy envy is quite common and is often overlooked or misdiagnosed. Envy is often confused with jealousy. Envy is unlike jealousy. Jealousy (as discussed in Chapter 6), is about a threat to your relationship with your partner from someone else. Envy is about someone having something or someone YOU desire. It could be said envy can be beneficial when it's healthy envy as it enables you to become aware of what you want; it can provoke aspirations, motivation and goal setting. However, in its unhealthy form it can be damaging and limiting, spoiling happiness and triggering other unhealthy negative emotions like anger, anxiety, depression and shame.

Unhealthy envy is provoked by unhealthy beliefs. A typical unhealthy envy provoking belief is as follows:

'My friend has a partner and a baby and we are of similar age. I must have what my friend has and because I don't it's intolerable, awful and makes me less worthy than I would be if I had what my friend has.'

Unhealthy envy often triggers problems of low self esteem and frustration due to the fact that we frequently compare ourselves to others in a self defeating way.

We have found that unhealthy envy is often experienced when one of your peers at work achieves something that you want to achieve or when someone gets pregnant, has a baby, starts a relationship or has the type of partner or lifestyle you want. This is more noticeable when the person who has the desired advantage is relatively similar to us. Unhealthy envy is more likely when the domain of comparison is very important to you, e.g. if you are interested in sport then you are more likely to be envious of a premier league footballer than someone who is a brilliant violinist.

Unhealthy envy can be a destructive emotion both mentally and physically. When you experience unhealthy envy you tend to also feel hostile, resentful, angry and irritable. You are also less able to be grateful about your positive traits and your circumstances.

Objects of Envy

We can be envious over other people's:

* possessions
* lifestyle
* qualifications
* looks
* success
* relationships
* fame.

The list could go on and on . . .

Shame and Unhealthy Envy

Shame is often experienced as a consequence of unhealthy envy. You do not find many people admitting to having unhealthy envy. If you are experiencing shame/embarrassment then you may need to work on your feelings of unhealthy envy as well as your feelings of shame. Shame is provoked by holding unhealthy beliefs about something negative revealed about you and being judged negatively for it, in this case being unhealthily envious. For example, 'I shouldn't be feeling envy or reveal to others that I am. If others know I'm envious they will judge me as bad and I agree with them because envy is a sign of badness.' If you are feeling shame about your feeling of envy then refer to Chapter 7.

Common Triggers for Unhealthy Envy

The following are common themes of unhealthy envy – the list is not exhaustive. Tick the boxes that you think apply to you.

Tick the box to identify your envy triggers

- ☐ Physical looks
- ☐ Age
- ☐ Youth
- ☐ Money
- ☐ Lifestyle
- ☐ Fertility
- ☐ Relationship
- ☐ Financial status
- ☐ Academic achievement or status
- ☐ Success
- ☐ Fortune
- ☐ Fame
- ☐ Talent
- ☐ Ability
- ☐ Family
- ☐ Community
- ☐ Culture
- ☐ Possessions
- ☐ Friendship
- ☐ Intelligence
- ☐ Career
- ☐ Happiness
- ☐ Luck
- ☐ Other (write your own reason)

Am I Healthily or Unhealthily Envious?

At the heart of your unhealthy envy are unhealthy beliefs about someone possessing something that you desire but do not have.

Such unhealthy beliefs not only provoke unhealthy envy but they have a consequence on how you think (cognitive consequences) and how you tend to behave (action tendencies). Behaviour is often an expression of the action tendencies.

When you feel unhealthy envy, for example, your thoughts may be preoccupied with 'it's not fair' or 'why shouldn't I have that?' or 'why should they have so much?'.

Assess if you are envious in a healthy or unhealthy way by checking your cognitive consequences and action tendencies.

Look through the illustrations for the cognitive consequences and action tendencies and work out if you are unhealthily envious or healthily envious. It is important to put yourself in the trigger situation when you feel or felt envious. It is easy to think that you don't have unhealthy thoughts when you are not triggered or when you are away from the trigger situation, so just imagine yourself in the frying pan, so to speak, and then work out if the envy is healthy or unhealthy.

Cognitive Consequences

Unhealthy Envy

You denigrate the value of the desired possession.

Cognitive Consequences

Healthy Envy

You honestly admit to yourself that you desire something.

Cognitive Consequences

Unhealthy Envy

You try to convince yourself that you are happy with your possession (although you are not).

Cognitive Consequences

Healthy Envy

You do not try to convince yourself that you are happy with your possession when you are not.

Cognitive Consequences

Unhealthy Envy

You think about how to acquire the desired possession regardless of its usefulness to you.

Cognitive Consequences

Healthy Envy

You think about how to obtain the desired possession because you desire it for healthy reasons.

Unhealthy Envy

You think about how to deprive the other person of the desired possession.

Cognitive Consequences

Healthy Envy

You can allow the other person to have and enjoy the desired possession without denigrating the person or the possession.

You belittle verbally the person who has the desired possession.

Action/Action Tendencies

Healthy Envy

You obtain the desired possession if it is truly what you want.

You verbally belittle the desired possession.

Healthy Envy

You do not verbally belittle the desired possession.

Action/Action Tendencies

Unhealthy Envy

You take away the desired possession from the other person (either to have it or to deprive the other person from having it).

Healthy Envy

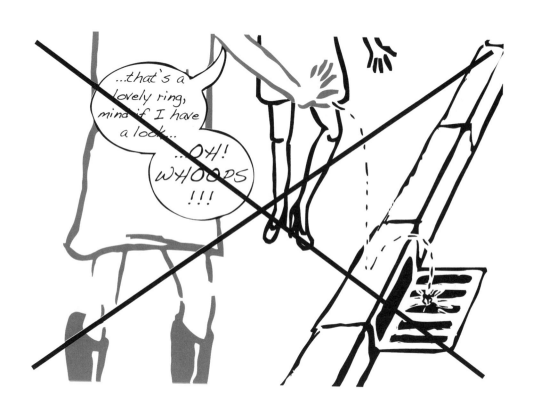

You do not take away the desired possession from the other person.

You spoil or destroy the desired possession so that the other
person does not have it.

Action/Action Tendencies

Healthy Envy

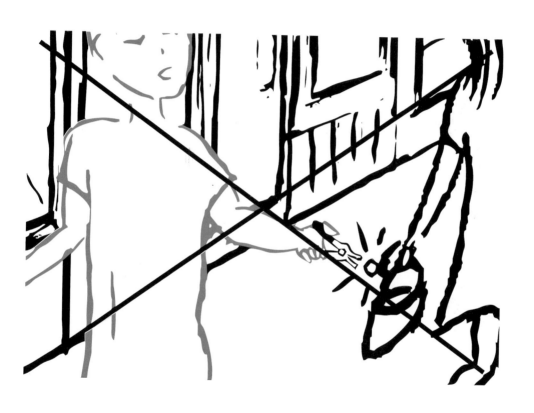

You do not spoil or destroy the desired possession so that
the other person does not have it.

Now . . .

General Change or Philosophical Change for you?

General Change

STEP 1   Choose a typical example of your unhealthy envy problem.

STEP 2   Identify your unhealthy envy cognitive consequences and action tendencies and write them in your own words, using the illustrations as a guide. Make sure that they are specific to your example.

STEP 3   Identify your healthy envy cognitive consequences and action tendencies and write them in your own words, using the illustrations as a guide. Make sure they are specific to your example.

STEP 4   Commit to thinking and behaving in accordance with your healthy cognitive consequences and action tendencies for healthy envy.

STEP 5   Repeat, Repeat, Repeat in a consistent and forceful manner until your new thinking and your new behaviour become second nature.

Tip:
If behaving in accordance with healthy envy is too overwhelming to begin with, then imagine yourself behaving in a healthy manner for a few weeks and then start in real life.

Philosophical Change

Remember to take your time if you are choosing this route, as Philosophical Change is about changing your unhealthy beliefs over the long term.

STEP 1   Identify your unhealthy belief.

STEP 2   Dispute your unhealthy belief.

STEP 3   Identify your healthy belief.

STEP 4   Dispute your healthy belief.

STEP 5   Strengthen your healthy belief and weaken your unhealthy belief.

Envy is provoked by unhealthy beliefs about someone else possessing something desirable that we do not have. Unhealthy beliefs are made up of absolutist **rigid beliefs** in the form of a MUST, HAVE TO, NEED TO, GOT TO, ABSOLUTELY SHOULD, from which three further derivative disturbed beliefs come.

AWFULISING BELIEF	LOW FRUSTRATION TOLERANCE BELIEF (LFT)	SELF DAMNING BELIEF
'It is awful.'	'It is unbearable.'	'It means I'm worthless.'

A
Event or Trigger
Most unhealthy envy
provoking event

B
Belief
Rigid belief and its
derivatives

C
Consequences
Unhealthy envy
Cognitive Consequences
Behaviour
Action Tendencies
Physical symptoms

A rigid belief, at **B**, is a demand about the most unhealthy envy provoking aspect of an event – it is a demand to **absolutely have what someone else has**.

For example, if what you are most unhealthily envious of is your friend's lifestyle, then the rigid belief is **I must have my friend's lifestyle**. The consequences of not having the rigid belief met are any or a combination of the three derivative beliefs.

For example:

RIGID BELIEF	AWFULISING BELIEF	LOW FRUSTRATION TOLERANCE BELIEF (LFT)	SELF DAMNING BELIEF
'My friend has a great lifestyle… I must have my friend's lifestyle.'	'The fact that I don't have my friend's lifestyle is awful.'	'The fact that I don't have my friend's lifestyle is unbearable.'	'If I don't have my friend's lifestyle it proves I am not as worthwhile as I would be if I had my friend's lifestyle.'

Step 1

Identify your unhealthy envy provoking belief

a. Choose a typical example of your unhealthy envy problem.

b. Use the previous Common Unhealthy Envy Triggers table as a reference to pinpoint what you were most envious about. You may have more than one trigger, which means you may have more than one unhealthy envy provoking belief. Work on one belief at a time.

c. Express your answer to Question (b) above in the form of a 'MUST'. (See above examples.)

d. Identify the derivative beliefs. (Awfulising, Low Frustration Tolerance (LFT), Self Damning. See page 5 as a reminder to what these mean.)

You may have all three derivatives or any combination of the three.

Remember to imagine yourself in the trigger situation when identifying these derivative beliefs.

Examples	A	LFT	SD/OD
'My friend has a partner and a baby and we are of similar age. I must have what my friend has and because I don't it's intolerable, awful and makes me less worthy than I would be if I had what my friend has.'	✓	✓	✓
'My colleague was just promoted. I must have what he has; I can't stand the fact that I don't.'		✓	
'My cousin is pregnant. I must have what she has; the fact that I'm not pregnant like my cousin is awful, unbearable.'	✓	✓	
'My partner is successful at work. I must be as successful as my partner. The fact that I'm not proves I'm not as worthwhile as I could be.'			✓

Key: A = Awfulising, LFT = Low Frustration Tolerance, SD = Self Damning,
OD = Other Damning

Step 2

dispute? your unhealthy envy provoking belief

Question the validity of your unhealthy belief using the following three criteria. Remember that an unhealthy belief is made up of the rigid belief and its derivatives. The disputing questions below are used on all of them:

a. Are they realistic or not and why?
b. Do they make sense or not and why?
c. Do they lead to helpful or unhelpful outcomes for me, and why?

Let's assume your unhealthy belief was as follows:

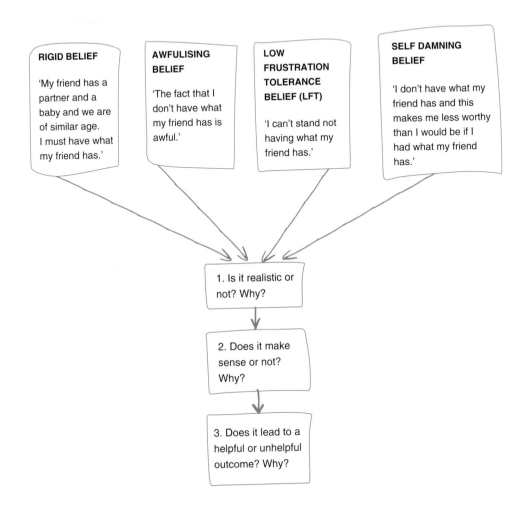

RIGID BELIEF

'My friend has a partner and a baby and we are of similar age. I must have what my friend has.'

AWFULISING BELIEF

'The fact that I don't have what my friend has is awful.'

LOW FRUSTRATION TOLERANCE BELIEF (LFT)

'I can't stand not having what my friend has.'

SELF DAMNING BELIEF

'I don't have what my friend has and this makes me less worthy than I would be if I had what my friend has.'

1. Is it realistic or not? Why?

2. Does it make sense or not? Why?

3. Does it lead to a helpful or unhelpful outcome? Why?

Go ahead and dispute your unhealthy belief or beliefs.

Step 3

Identify your healthy envy provoking belief

a. Change your unhealthy belief and work out the healthy version by removing the rigidity and replacing it with the preference belief.

b. Remember to negate your unhealthy demand. For example, 'I want what my friend has BUT I absolutely don't have to have it'.

c. Identify the derivative beliefs (Anti-awfulising, High Frustration Tolerance (HFT), Self/Other/World Acceptance. See page 7 as a reminder to what these mean.) Use the examples below as a guide.

d. Remember, preference beliefs are flexible, make sense and lead to a helpful outcome.

Unhealthy beliefs	A	LFT	SD/OD
'My friend has a partner and a baby and we are of similar age. I must have what my friend has because if I don't it's intolerable, awful and makes me less worthy than I would be if I had what my friend has.'	✓	✓	✓
'My colleague was just promoted. I must have what he has; I can't stand the fact that I don't.'		✓	
'My cousin is pregnant. I must have what she has; the fact that I'm not pregnant like my cousin is awful, unbearable.'	✓	✓	
'My partner is successful at work. I must be as successful as my partner; the fact that I'm not proves I'm not as worthwhile as I could be.'			✓

Healthy versions	AA	HFT	SA/OA
'My friend has a partner and a baby and we are of similar age. I want to have what my friend has but I don't have to. The fact that I don't is frustrating but not intolerable, bad but not awful; it doesn't me make less worthwhile. I am worthwhile regardless.'	✓	✓	✓
'My colleague was just promoted. I want what he has but it doesn't mean that I absolutely must. I can stand the fact that I don't even though it's hard.'		✓	
'My cousin is pregnant. I want to have what she has but I absolutely don't have to have it. The fact that I'm not pregnant like my cousin is bad but not awful, difficult but not unbearable.'	✓	✓	
'My partner is successful at work. I want to be as successful as my partner but I don't have to be; the fact that I'm not does not prove I'm not as worthwhile. I'm worthwhile regardless.'			✓

Key: A = Awfulising, LFT = Low Frustration Tolerance, SD = Self Damning,
OD = Other Damning, AA = Anti Awfulising, HFT = High Frustration Tolerance,
SA = Self Acceptance, OA = Other Acceptance

Go ahead and rewrite your beliefs in a healthy way.

Step 4

dispute? your healthy envy provoking belief

Dispute your healthy beliefs using the same criteria used in disputing the unhealthy beliefs – this keeps it fair and you are more likely to persuade yourself to commit to changing them if you dispute the unhealthy and the healthy beliefs in exactly the same way.

Remember that a healthy belief is made up of a preference belief and its three balanced derivatives or a combination of them. The disputing questions below are used on all of them.

HEALTHY BELIEF

'My friend has a partner and a baby and we are of similar age. I want to have what my friend has but I don't have to.'

ANTI-AWFULISING BELIEF

'The fact that I don't have what my friend has is bad but not awful.'

HIGH FRUSTRATION TOLERANCE BELIEF (HFT)

'The fact that I don't have what my friend has is difficult but not intolerable.'

SELF ACCEPTANCE BELIEF

'That fact that I don't have what my friend has doesn't make me less worthwhile. I accept myself as worthwhile regardless.'

1. Is it realistic or not? Why?

2. Does it make sense or not? Why?

3. Does it lead to a helpful or unhelpful outcome? Why?

Tip:
Remember that anti-awfulising is where 100% bad does not exist, as one can usually think of something worse.

Tip:
HFT means you have not disintegrated.

Tip:
Self/other acceptance is not dependent on conditions. We are all fallible human beings.

Go ahead and dispute your healthy belief and its balanced derivatives.

Step 5

STRENGTHEN your healthy envy provoking belief

weaken your unhealthy envy provoking belief

In order to change your unhealthy envy provoking beliefs to healthy envy beliefs, you need to think in accordance with your healthy belief and take constructive actions. The illustrations demonstrate the thinking (cognitive consequences) and the action tendencies of healthy envy. The constructive actions are based on the action tendencies of healthy envy.

- Think and act in accordance with your healthy belief repeatedly and consistently in a forceful manner until eventually your emotional state changes from unhealthy envy to healthy envy.

- Remember your emotion of unhealthy envy **will** change – the new way of thinking and the new actions you will implement will feel uncomfortable initially but this is completely natural. You are changing an old habit of unhealthy thinking and old habitual unhealthy envy behaviours. It takes a few weeks of repetitions done consistently and forcefully.

- The behavioural goals you set for yourself need to be challenging but not overwhelming. If you overwhelm yourself then it defeats the object of the exercise.

- Start with imagining yourself thinking and acting in a healthy manner whilst being in the trigger situation until you think you are ready to challenge yourself in real life. For example, you may set a goal that whilst socialising with friends you only express healthy emotional responses about other people's good fortune (rather than your usual unhealthy envy provoked comments) and then continue until you achieve your desired goal.

- Repeat your healthy belief in your head daily and particularly when you are imagining yourself in the trigger situation. This mental rehearsal will help you to remember it when you deliberately face the trigger situation in real life.

- Once you achieve your desired goal, whatever it is, then you need to maintain the helpful thinking and actions.

- Review how you did, each time you challenge yourself, then work out what you can do differently or better the next time. Then do it. Do not demand perfection from yourself. The process of moving from unhealthy envy to healthy envy is uncomfortable and uneven. Some days you will make bigger strides when you challenge yourself and other days you will make small strides or even take a step back. The important thing is to accept that this can happen and then bring your focus back to what you are doing and continue with it.

- Remember, you didn't learn to drive a car, ride a bicycle or learn to read overnight, it takes repetition and focus and consistency.

Chapter 8 – Envy – Takeaway Tips

- Self awareness: practise examining your thoughts to determine whether you feel healthy or unhealthy envy. If you find that they are triggering unhealthy envy, remind yourself of how these thoughts don't help your life and can actually harm it. The more you can manage to catch and correct your thinking, the easier it will be to remain in a state of healthy envy.

- Become more self aware by noticing your behaviours and correcting them.

- Act towards others in a way you would like to be treated yourself. Remember, you are not avoiding experiencing healthy envy.

- Take time to set goals in your life and create your own aspirations, allowing other people's lives to inform you in a helpful, healthily envious way.

Theoretical Perspectives on Cognitive Behaviour Therapy

Albert Ellis and Aaron Beck

At the beginning of the book, we touched on the two pioneers of CBT, Albert Ellis and Aaron Beck. We will now briefly explain the two main schools of Cognitive Behaviour Therapy. Both have a scientific theory that can be, and has been, tested as well as a structured framework and process of therapy.

The Ellis Model

Rational Emotive Behaviour Therapy was founded in 1955 by Albert Ellis and has the longest history of any of the cognitive behaviour therapies. This book has focused on using Ellis's model because of its humanistic robust theory and philosophical basis.

REBT, as covered in the book, can be conceptualised by the ABC diagram below, where it is not the event, but the belief or view you hold about the event, which is at the heart of emotional states.

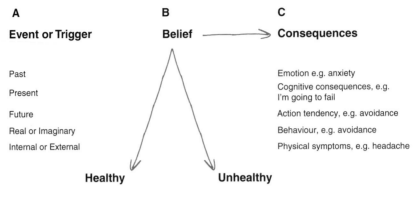

CBT, Event, Belief, Consequences Diagram

Ellis's REBT is about helping people to:

1. Understand their emotions, behaviour and goals.
2. Identify their unhealthy or unhelpful beliefs that are sabotaging their happiness and goals.
3. Challenge them and replace them with their healthier version in order to become undisturbed and eventually happy through consistent and constructive action.

It helps us develop resiliency and self acceptance by enabling us to face our disturbances full on rather than ignoring them through distraction and avoidance. This can lead to a powerful philosophical shift which focuses us on our desires, wants and wishes without becoming disturbed about our past, present or future setbacks. We learn to view setbacks and failures as purely temporary as opposed to life or soul destroying, while remaining motivated and focused on our desires and goals.

The Beck Model

Beck's model is called Cognitive Therapy (CT). It says that our emotions and behaviour are influenced by the way we think and by how we make sense of the world. Our interpretations and assumptions developed from personal experience often conflict with the real world. Beck encouraged his patients to focus their attention on their 'automatic thoughts'.

Clients are helped to test their assumptions and views of the world in order to check if they fit with reality. When clients learn that their perceptions and interpretations are distorted or unhelpful they then work at correcting them.

Differences between the Ellis and Beck Models

Both schools are open to influence from each other and, in practice, ideas from both can be utilised, as appropriate, to achieve successful outcomes for clients. However, they remain distinct. The main distinctions are i) testing assumptions and ii) philosophical basis.

Testing Assumptions

In Ellis's model the client's assumptions are assumed to be true and are not immediately put to a reality test. In Beck's model the client's assumptions are tested for validity first. The reason for this is that REBT theory states that a client's assumptions are a consequence of holding unhealthy beliefs, so these assumptions are assumed to be true in order to 'cut to the chase' and identify the unhealthy beliefs.

Treating Symptoms or Generalised Philosophy?

Beck's model is based on the treatment of the symptom. REBT treats the symptom but its aim is to effect 'profound philosophic change and a radically new outlook on life' (Albert Ellis) by transforming deeply held core beliefs about the self, others and the world.

However, a drawback to REBT may be that some people may not like its direct approach. Beck's model is more cautious and aims for some kind of improvement and return to normal functioning, symptom relief or symptom management. On the negative side, this approach misses the chance to offer people a simple philosophy and the tools to become their own therapists when faced with different problems in the future. Our preference is REBT.

Ellis or Beck? That is the Question . . .

Both were great thinkers and have made an enormous contribution to the understanding and application of psychological health.

Glossary of Terms

Action Tendencies – The way we feel like acting. Action tendencies are influenced by the beliefs we hold; they can be self defeating or constructive.

Anger – An unhealthy negative emotion provoked by unhealthy beliefs about the breaking of a non moral rule. Its healthy counterpart is annoyance.

Anti-awfulising – Negative events are placed on a scale of 0–99.9% badness where 100% bad does not exist, as one can usually think of something worse.

Anxiety – An unhealthy negative emotion provoked by unhealthy beliefs about a real or perceived threat. Its healthy negative emotion counterpart is concern.

Awfulising – An unrealistic assessment of *badness* where negative events are viewed or defined as 'end of the world bad' or 100% or more bad, e.g. 'it would be awful if I'm rejected', 'it would be the end of the world if I am rejected and therefore I must not be rejected'.

Behaviours – Actions we take. We usually behave in accordance with the action tendencies but not always.

Belief – A fully evaluative thought that is centrally involved in our emotional experiences. Musts and Preferences, Awfulising and Anti-awfulising, Low Frustration Tolerance and High Frustration Tolerance, Self/Other/World Damning and Self/Other/World Acceptance are evaluative because they point to what we believe is true and accurate.

Cognitive Behaviour Therapy – A form of psychotherapy that focuses on two areas: the way that you think (cognitive) and the things that you do (behaviour). The two pioneers of CBT, Albert Ellis and Aaron Beck, shared the view that most emotional problems arise from faulty thinking and that the remedy is to be found in corrective actions. Both the Ellis and Beck approaches concentrate on *present* problems and *present* thinking in contrast to the earlier forms of psychotherapy.

Cognitive Consequences – The thoughts we have related to the beliefs we hold. Beliefs can be either healthy or unhealthy.

Concern – A healthy negative emotion provoked by healthy beliefs about a threat, either perceived or real. It is the healthy counterpart of anxiety.

Concern for One's Relationship – A healthy negative emotion provoked by healthy beliefs about a real or perceived threat to your relationship by a third party. The unhealthy counterpart is jealousy.

Depression – An unhealthy negative emotion provoked by unhealthy beliefs about loss or failure. Its healthy counterpart is sadness.

Disappointment – A healthy negative emotion provoked by healthy beliefs about being treated insensitively. Its unhealthy counterpart is hurt.

Disputing – A process of questioning unhealthy and healthy beliefs against three criteria. Is it consistent with reality? Does it make sense? Does it help?

Embarrassment – An unhealthy negative emotion provoked by unhealthy beliefs about something negative being revealed about you, or a group you associate yourself with, and the perceived or real consequential shunning by others. Its healthy counterpart is Regret.

Emotional Disturbance – A term to describe an unhealthy negative emotional experience. It is provoked by holding unhealthy beliefs about adverse events. Emotional Disturbance can also be viewed as being emotionally stuck.

Emotional Responsibility – The principle that your feelings and reactions are greatly influenced by the attitudes and beliefs that you currently hold as true.

Envy – An unhealthy negative emotion provoked by unhealthy beliefs about wanting some possession that someone else has. Its healthy counterpart is healthy envy.

Guilt – An unhealthy negative emotion provoked by unhealthy beliefs about you transgressing your own moral rule. Its healthy counterpart is remorse.

Healthy Beliefs – Beliefs that are healthy have, at their core, preferences, usually expressed as wants and desires. Preferences, Anti Awfulising, High Frustration Tolerance, Self/Other/World Acceptance are healthy beliefs. They are consistent with reality, logical and promote psychological health.

Healthy Envy – A healthy negative emotion provoked by healthy beliefs about wanting a possession that someone else already has. Its unhealthy counterpart is unhealthy envy.

Healthy Negative Emotions – Emotions that are experienced when we hold healthy beliefs about negative or adverse events.

High Frustration Tolerance (HFT) – A healthy belief about the ability to tolerate frustration or difficulty.

Hurt – An unhealthy negative emotion provoked by unhealthy beliefs about being treated insensitively. Its healthy counterpart is sorrow or disappointment.

Jealousy – An unhealthy negative emotion provoked by unhealthy beliefs about a real or perceived threat to your relationship by a third party. Its healthy counterpart is concern for one's relationship.

Low Frustration Tolerance (LFT) – An unhealthy belief about your perceived inability to tolerate frustration or difficulty.

Negative Emotions – These are the natural emotions we experience in relation to adverse life events, whether real or imaginary, rather than positive emotions. Negative emotions can be healthy or unhealthy.

REBT – One of the Cognitive Behaviour Therapies developed by Albert Ellis.

Regret – A healthy negative emotion provoked by healthy beliefs about something negative being revealed about you or a group you associate yourself with and the perceived or real consequential shunning by others. Its unhealthy counterpart is shame/embarrassment.

Remorse – A healthy negative emotion provoked by healthy beliefs about breaking your own moral code. Its unhealthy counterpart is guilt.

Sadness – A healthy negative emotion provoked by healthy beliefs about loss or failure. Its unhealthy counterpart is depression.

Self – The total of every conceivable thing about you. This includes all your behaviours since birth, all the emotions you have ever felt, all the thoughts, images, fantasies you have ever had, your values and your psychological and biological makeup.

Self/Other/World Damning – It is an unhealthy belief, it means rating the self, another person or the world in a totally negative way based on a condition. For example, 'if I fail, then I am a total failure', 'you are a totally bad person because you acted badly', 'the world is a totally awful place because bad things happen'.

Self Esteem – The rating or judging of the self. Esteem is from the verb 'to estimate'. Self esteem can go up and down and is therefore flawed as a concept.

Self Worth – The acceptance of the self based on the fact that all human beings are worthwhile just because they exist. It is a form of unconditional positive regard.

Shame – An unhealthy negative emotion provoked by unhealthy beliefs about something negative being revealed about you or a group you associate yourself with and the perceived or real consequential shunning by others. Its healthy counterpart is Regret.

Unconditional Self/Other/World Acceptance – Unconditional acceptance of self, others or the world is a healthy belief. It means accepting yourself, another or the world as fallible or imperfect. For example, acceptance of self is not dependent on conditions such as approval or love.

Unhealthy Beliefs – Have, at their core, explicit or implicit, rigid, powerful demands usually expressed as MUSTs, SHOULDs, HAVE TOs, GOT TOs, e.g. *I absolutely must not be rejected*. Demands, Awfulising, LFT and Self/Other/World Damning are unhealthy beliefs. They are rigid, inconsistent with reality, illogical and promote psychological disturbance.

Useful Organisations

Alcoholics Anonymous
Web: www.alcoholics-anonymous.org.uk

Association for Rational Emotive Behaviour Therapy (AREBT)
Web: www.arebt.org

British Association of Anger Management (BAAM)
Tel: 0845 1300 286
Web: www.angermanage.co.uk

British Association for Behavioural and Cognitive Psychotherapies (BABCP)
Web: www.babcp.com

British Association for Counselling and Psychotherapy (BACP)
Web: www.bacp.co.uk

Cruse Bereavement Care
Helpline: 0844 477 9400
Web: crusebereavementcare.org.uk
Email: info@cruse.org.uk

Depression Alliance
Tel: 0845 123 2320
Web: www.depressionalliance.org
Information and support for anyone affected by depression

Depression Support Network (DEPEND)

Web: www.dep-end.org
Email: depaware@hotmail.com

Everyman Project

Helpline: 020 7263 8884
Web: www.everymanproject.co.uk
Counselling for men who want to stop their violence

MIND

Web: www.mind.org.uk
Email: contact@mind.org.uk

Samaritans

Web: www.samaritans.org
Email: jo@samaritans.org

SANE

Web: www.sane.org.uk
Email: info@sane.org.uk

Supportline

Web: www.supportline.org.uk
Helpline for problems, including child abuse, bullying,
depression, anxiety, domestic violence and sexual assault

Women's Aid

Helpline: 0808 2000 247
Web: www.womensaid.org.uk
Email: helpline@womensaid.org.uk
National domestic violence charity

YoungMinds

Web: www.youngminds.org.uk

Acknowledgements

To our students who provoked the initial idea for the book.

To all our clients who have informed our work over the years.

Maggie to her sons Massih and Remi, and their refreshing perspectives on life.

We would like to acknowledge all the wonderful support and input from Holly Bennion and Jenny Ng at John Wiley and Sons Ltd – they have been amazing.

Professor Windy Dryden for his support and guidance.

My mother, Mrs L Joseph.

About the Authors

Avy Joseph

Avy is a Director and Co-founder of the College of Cognitive Behavioural Therapies (CCBT) and City Minds. He is a registered and accredited CBT therapist with the AREBT and the BABCP and runs a busy clinic in central London.

He gained a Masters degree in Rational-Emotive Behavioural Therapy, one of the main schools of Cognitive Behaviour Therapy from Goldsmiths College, University of London in 2001. He graduated with a degree in mathematics, after which he qualified as a counsellor and then worked in the private sector for many years in training and development. He has lectured both nationally and internationally.

Over the years he has developed many workshops and courses that have culminated in the development of specialised courses at the CCBT.

Maggie Chapman

Maggie is a Director and Co-founder of CCBT and City Minds. She is an experienced therapist who, over the years, has developed an integrative approach to her work, employing Cognitive Behaviour Therapy and brief solution focused strategies.

With degrees in business and psychology, Maggie qualified as an accountant working in the City, giving her an insight into the stresses relating to the corporate environment. She then went on to qualify as a bereavement and trauma counsellor before further developing her skills to work with adolescents.

She has lectured for many years both nationally and internationally and developed many courses, seminars and workshops. She has private practices in central and south west London.

Patrick Watkinson (illustrator)

Patrick trained as a Stage Manager at RADA and later Theatre Design at the Slade School of Fine Art UCL. He has had an eclectic career which has included production design for music videos, new plays and large stadium operas. Patrick's most recent work includes designing with Jamie Hewlett and Gorillaz their Opera *Monkey: Journey to the West* (Manchester International Festival, the Theatre du Châtelet Paris, 2007, and the O2, 2008). Patrick is currently designing contemporary circus productions for The Generating Company.